Francis Frith's
DOWN THE SEVERN

PHOTOGRAPHIC MEMORIES

Francis Frith's
DOWN THE SEVERN

───────◆───────

Clive Hardy

FRITH
BOOK Co

First published in the United Kingdom in 2000 by
Frith Book Company Ltd

Hardback Edition 2000
ISBN 1-85937-118-3

Reprinted in Hardback 2001 & 2002
ISBN 1-85937-118-3

Paperback Edition 2002
ISBN 1-85937-560-x

British Library Cataloguing in Publication Data

Francis Frith's Down The Severn
Clive Hardy

Frith Book Company Ltd
Frith's Barn, Teffont,
Salisbury, Wiltshire SP3 5QP
Tel: +44 (0) 1722 716 376
Email: info@francisfrith.co.uk
www.francisfrith.co.uk

Printed and bound in Great Britain

Contents

Francis Frith: Victorian Pioneer

FRANCIS FRITH, Victorian founder of the world-famous photographic archive, was a complex and multi-talented man. A devout Quaker and a highly successful Victorian businessman, he was both philosophic by nature and pioneering in outlook.

By 1855 Francis Frith had already established a wholesale grocery business in Liverpool, and sold it for the astonishing sum of £200,000, which is the equivalent today of over £15,000,000. Now a multi-millionaire, he was able to indulge his passion for travel. As a child he had pored over travel books written by early explorers, and his fancy and imagination had been stirred by family holidays to the sublime mountain regions of Wales and Scotland. 'What a land of spirit-stirring and enriching scenes and places!' he had written. He was to return to these scenes of grandeur in later years to 'recapture the thousands of vivid and tender memories', but with a different purpose. Now in his thirties, and captivated by the new science of photography, Frith set out on a series of pioneering journeys to the Nile regions that occupied him from 1856 until 1860.

Intrigue and Adventure

He took with him on his travels a specially-designed wicker carriage that acted as both dark-room and sleeping chamber. These far-flung journeys were packed with intrigue and adventure. In his life story, written when he was sixty-three, Frith tells of being held captive by bandits, and of fighting 'an awful midnight battle to the very point of surrender with a deadly pack of hungry, wild dogs'. Sporting flowing Arab costume, Frith arrived at Akaba by camel seventy years before Lawrence, where he encountered 'desert princes and rival sheikhs, blazing with jewel-hilted swords'.

During these extraordinary adventures he was assiduously exploring the desert regions bordering the Nile and patiently recording the antiquities and peoples with his camera. He was the first photographer to venture beyond the sixth cataract. Africa was still the mysterious 'Dark Continent', and Stanley and Livingstone's historic meeting was a decade into the future. The conditions for picture taking confound belief. He laboured for hours in his wicker dark-room in the sweltering heat of the desert, while the volatile chemicals fizzed dangerously in their trays. Often he was forced to work in remote tombs and caves where conditions were cooler. Back in London he exhibited his photographs and was 'rapturously cheered' by members of the Royal Society. His reputation as a photographer was made overnight. An eminent modern historian has likened their impact on the population of the time to that on our own generation of the first photographs taken on the surface of the moon.

Venture of a Life-Time

Characteristically, Frith quickly spotted the opportunity to create a new business as a specialist publisher of photographs. He lived in an era of immense and sometimes violent change. For the poor in the early part of Victoria's reign work was a drudge and the hours long, and people had precious little free time to enjoy themselves. Most had no transport other than a cart or gig at their disposal, and had not travelled far beyond the boundaries of their own town or village. However,

by the 1870s, the railways had threaded their way across the country, and Bank Holidays and half-day Saturdays had been made obligatory by Act of Parliament. All of a sudden the ordinary working man and his family were able to enjoy days out and see a little more of the world.

With characteristic business acumen, Francis Frith foresaw that these new tourists would enjoy having souvenirs to commemorate their days out. In 1860 he married Mary Ann Rosling and set out with the intention of photographing every city, town and village in Britain. For the next thirty years he travelled the country by train and by pony and trap, producing fine photographs of seaside resorts and beauty spots that were keenly bought by millions of Victorians. These prints were painstakingly pasted into family albums and pored over during the dark nights of winter, rekindling precious memories of summer excursions.

The Rise of Frith & Co

Frith's studio was soon supplying retail shops all over the country. To meet the demand he gathered about him a small team of photographers, and published the work of independent artist-photographers of the calibre of Roger Fenton and Francis Bedford. In order to gain some understanding of the scale of Frith's business one only has to look at the catalogue issued by Frith & Co in 1886: it runs to some 670 pages, listing not only many thousands of views of the British Isles but also many photographs of most European countries, and China, Japan, the USA and Canada – note the sample page shown above from the hand-written *Frith & Co* ledgers detailing pictures taken. By 1890 Frith had created the greatest specialist photographic publishing company in the

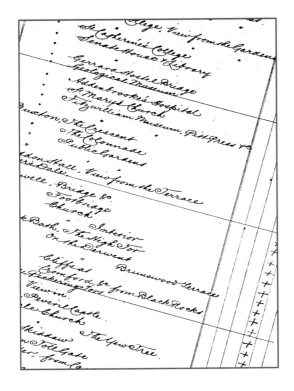

year after Frith's death, a new card measuring 5.5 x 3.5 inches became the standard format, but it was not until 1902 that the divided back came into being, with address and message on one face and a full-size illustration on the other. *Frith & Co* were in the vanguard of postcard development, and Frith's sons Eustace and Cyril continued their father's monumental task, expanding the number of views offered to the public and recording more and more places in Britain, as the coasts and countryside were opened up to mass travel.

Francis Frith died in 1898 at his villa in Cannes, his great project still growing. The archive he created continued in business for another seventy years. By 1970 it contained over a third of a million pictures of 7,000 cities, towns and villages. The massive photographic record Frith has left to us stands as a living monument to a special and very remarkable man.

world, with over 2,000 outlets more than the combined number that Boots and W H Smith have today! The picture on the right shows the *Frith & Co* display board at Ingleton in the Yorkshire Dales. Beautifully constructed with mahogany frame and gilt inserts, it could display up to a dozen local scenes.

Postcard Bonanza

The ever-popular holiday postcard we know today took many years to develop. In 1870 the Post Office issued the first plain cards, with a pre-printed stamp on one face. In 1894 they allowed other publishers' cards to be sent through the mail with an attached adhesive halfpenny stamp. Demand grew rapidly, and in 1895 a new size of postcard was permitted called the court card, but there was little room for illustration. In 1899, a

Frith's Archive: A Unique Legacy

FRANCIS FRITH'S legacy to us today is of immense significance and value, for the magnificent archive of evocative photographs he created provides a unique record of change in 7,000 cities, towns and villages throughout Britain over a century and more. Frith and his fellow studio photographers revisited locations many times down the years to update their views, compiling for us an enthralling and colourful pageant of British life and character.

We tend to think of Frith's sepia views of Britain as nostalgic, for most of us use them to conjure up memories of places in our own lives with which we have family associations. It often makes us forget that to Francis Frith they were records of daily life as it was actually being lived in the cities, towns and villages of his day. The Victorian age was one of great and often bewildering change for ordinary people, and though the pictures evoke an impression of slower times, life was as busy and hectic as it is today.

We are fortunate that Frith was a photographer of the people, dedicated to recording the minutiae of everyday life. For it is this sheer wealth of visual data, the painstaking chronicle of changes in dress, transport, street layouts, buildings, housing, engineering and landscape that captivates us so much today. His remarkable images offer us a powerful link with the past and with the lives of our ancestors.

Today's Technology

Computers have now made it possible for Frith's many thousands of images to be accessed almost instantly. In the Frith archive today, each photograph is carefully 'digitised' then stored on a CD Rom. Frith archivists can locate a single photograph amongst thousands within seconds. Views can be catalogued and sorted under a variety of categories of place and content to the immediate benefit of researchers.

Inexpensive reference prints can be created for them at the touch of a mouse button, and a wide range of books and other printed materials assembled and published for a wider, more general readership - in the next twelve months over a hundred Frith local history titles will be published! The day-to-day workings of the archive are very different from how they were in Francis Frith's time: imagine the herculean task of sorting through eleven tons of glass negatives as Frith had to do to locate a particular sequence of pictures!

THE FRANCIS FRITH COLLECTION

Photographic publishers since 1860

| HOME | PHOTO SEARCH | BOOKS | PORTFOLIO | GALLERY | | MY CART |

| Products | History | Other Collections | Contact us | Help? |

your town,
your village

365,000 photographs of 7,000 towns and villages, taken between 1860 & 1970.

The Frith Archive

The Frith Archive is the remarkable legacy of its energetic and visionary founder. Today, the Frith archive is the only nationally important archive of its kind still in private ownership.

The Collection is world-renowned for the extraordinary quality of its images.

The Gallery

This month The Frith Gallery features images from "Frith's Egypt".

*the*FRITHgallery

News...

Image update complete. An additional 5,000 images have been added and the quality of all images has now been improved.

Sample Chapters available. The first selection of sample chapters from the Frith Book Co.'s extensive range is now available. All are offered in Pdf format for easy downloading and viewing.

explore
FRITH
Search thousands of photographs from one of the worlds' great archives.

Town search
[ ] GO

County search
[Select a county ▼] GO

See Frith at www.francisfrith.co.uk

Yet the archive still prides itself on maintaining the same high standards of excellence laid down by Francis Frith, including the painstaking cataloguing and indexing of every view.

It is curious to reflect on how the internet now allows researchers in America and elsewhere greater instant access to the archive than Frith himself ever enjoyed. Many thousands of individual views can be called up on screen within seconds on one of the Frith internet sites, enabling people living continents away to revisit the streets of their ancestral home town, or view places in Britain where they have enjoyed holidays. Many overseas researchers welcome the chance to view special theme selections, such as transport, sports, costume and ancient monuments.

We are certain that Francis Frith would have heartily approved of these modern developments in imaging techniques, for he himself was always working at the very limits of Victorian photographic technology.

The Value of the Archive Today

Because of the benefits brought by the computer, Frith's images are increasingly studied by social historians, by researchers into genealogy and ancestory, by architects, town planners, and by teachers and schoolchildren involved in local history projects.

In addition, the archive offers every one of us an opportunity to examine the places where we and our families have lived and worked down the years. Highly successful in Frith's own era, the archive is now, a century and more on, entering a new phase of popularity.

The Past in Tune with the Future

Historians consider the Francis Frith Collection to be of prime national importance. It is the only archive of its kind remaining in private ownership and has been valued at a million pounds. However, this figure is now rapidly increasing as digital technology enables more and more people around the world to enjoy its benefits.

Francis Frith's archive is now housed in an historic timber barn in the beautiful village of Teffont in Wiltshire. Its founder would not recognize the archive office as it is today. In place of the many thousands of dusty boxes containing glass plate negatives and an all-pervading odour of photographic chemicals, there are now ranks of computer screens. He would be amazed to watch his images travelling round the world at unimaginable speeds through network and internet lines.

The archive's future is both bright and exciting. Francis Frith, with his unshakeable belief in making photographs available to the greatest number of people, would undoubtedly approve of what is being done today with his lifetime's work. His photographs, depicting our shared past, are now bringing pleasure and enlightenment to millions around the world a century and more after his death.

DOWN THE SEVERN
An Introduction

Rising 2000 ft above sea level upon the wild slopes of Plynlimon in Powys, the Severn at 220 miles in length is the longest river in British Isles; it was once navigable from where it joins the Bristol Channel to Welshpool, 128 miles up river from Gloucester. In this book we look at some of the places the river flows through on its somewhat meandering course to the sea.

In this selection the earliest picture is of Shrewsbury: the photograph of Wyle Cop was taken in 1891. This is a steep street that connects the High Street with the English Bridge. It was along here in a half-timbered house near the top that Henry Tudor spent the night before riding on to defeat Richard III at Bosworth and take the throne. Like Durham, Shrewsbury was founded on a peninsula of high ground almost surrounded by water. For centuries this important strategic site and crossing point was fought for in turn by Welsh patriots, rebellious barons, Roundheads and Royalists. In 1283 Edward Longshanks, probably the most ruthless and

yet most able king ever to sit upon the throne of England, brought Dafydd ap Gruffydd, the last native Welsh prince, to Shrewsbury to be tried, condemned and hung, drawn and quartered. From Shrewsbury our journey continues by way of Atcham, with its parish church dedicated to St Eata and its seven-arched bridge designed by John Gywnne, to the ruins of the Cistercian abbey at Buildwas, and from there to Madeley and Ironbridge.

Abraham Darby probably chose Coalbrookdale for the location of his ironworks because there were local sources of coal and iron ore, and sufficient water power to work the bellows of his blast furnace. Darby was also able to export his products by way of the Severn. He was smelting with coke as early as 1709, yet it would be over fifty years before other ironmasters followed suit. Largely financed by Quaker merchants from Bristol, the Coalbrookdale works became famous in 1779 when Abraham Darby II manufactured the castings for the first bridge in the world to be made of iron. Weighing 380 tons, the single-arched structure, with a span of 100 ft and overall length of 196 ft, was floated down the river in sections and assembled in situ without obstructing other river traffic. The place where it was erected was named after it: Ironbridge. From Ironbridge we make our way to Worcester, calling in at a number of places including Bridgnorth, Bewdley, Stourport-on-Severn, and Holt Fleet.

When James Brindley was surveying the route for the Staffordshire & Worcestershire Canal, his original intention had been to make the junction with the Severn at Bewdley, which was already a flourishing up-river port. For reasons best known to themselves, the local natives were hostile, and Brindley had to look elsewhere. The place he found was the sleepy hamlet of Lower Mitton, just four miles down-river. Stourport, as Little Mitton became known, was a product of the Canal Age; boatyards, warehouses and interchange facilities for canal and river traffic attracted other industries. Soon there were spinning mills, an iron foundry, vinegar works and carpet mills. As Stourport prospered, Bewdley died the death of a thousand cuts. By the beginning of the 19th century, keeping the Severn north of Bewdley open to navigation was becoming more and more difficult. Barges for Coalbrookdale had to be bow-hauled from Bewdley by gangs of men, and when this practice finally died out Bewdley was finished. By the 1900s, only craft drawing less than 21 inches of water could attempt the river north of Stourport, and even then a shoal about one mile south of Bewdley barred further progress.

Worcester, home of the Royal Porcelain Works, Lea & Perrins, and a magnificent cathedral where King John and Prince Arthur, the elder brother of Henry VIII, are buried, also played a major role in the English Civil

BRIDGNORTH, THE BRIDGE 1898 42624

War. On 23 September 1642 the first serious clash between the Royalists and Parliamentarians took place near Powick Bridge, where in a brief skirmish Prince Rupert defeated Colonel John Brown. In 1651 Charles II raised his Royal Standard at Worcester during his attempt to win back his throne. Worcester had supported his late father during the earlier wars; because of this, Gloucester, where he gained a reputation for resilience and unorthodox tactics, mounting daring raids upon neighbouring Royalist garrisons. Massey realised that the bridge over the Severn at Upton posed a serious threat to Charles. Whilst leading a raid to destroy it, Massey was seriously injured; Charles was thereby denied the services of an outstanding soldier.

UPTON-ON-SEVERN 1931 84660

Charles hoped that it would be a centre of resistance against Parliament. Also it was the nearest substantial place to London that did not have a Parliamentarian garrison. Within days, however, Parliament had committed 28,000 troops to the campaign, and soon had Charles bottled up within the city. A former Parliamentarian officer who offered his sword to Charles was none other than Edward Massey. Massey had commanded the beleaguered Parliamentarian forces at

The next important place down river is Tewkesbury, which is situated on the confluence of the Severn and the Avon. The town is noted for its abbey, which was originally founded in c715, many fine half-timbered buildings, and the location of one of the bloodiest battles of the Wars of the Roses. On 14 May 1471 an exhausted Lancastrian army took up its position for battle in the sweltering heat; its back was to Swillgate brook, its front faced the Gloucester road. Though they outnumbered the Yorkists, the Lancastrians were in no fit state to fight; they had just made a forced march from Weymouth, where they had landed with Queen Margaret. To compound their suffering further, they had been denied food, rest and shelter at Gloucester, where Sir Richard Beauchamp had closed the gates against them. Both sides were arrayed in three divisions. The Lancastrian left was commanded by Lord Somerset, the centre by Lord Wenlock, a defector from the Yorkists, and Prince Edward; the right was under the Earl of Devonshire. Richard, Duke of Gloucester commanded the Yorkist left, King Edward IV the centre, and Lord Hastings the right. Somerset attacked first, launching an assault against Gloucester's division. Gloucester fell back, but this was purely a feint in order to enable Yorkist troops to get behind Somerset's men and attack them from the rear. Chaos ensued. Had Wenlock moved to support Somerset, the outcome might have been different, but he stayed put. The Yorkists pressed home their advantage, and Somerset's men were routed. The Lancastrian army crumbled. Somerset, who had always suspected Wenlock's motives for changing sides, went up to the noble lord and caved his skull in with his mace. Defeated Lancastrians sought sanctuary in the abbey, where Abbot Strensham was holding Mass. Led by Edward IV, the Yorkists entered the abbey and began slaughtering the Lancastrians. Abbot Strensham demanded the killing be stopped, whereupon a number of Lancastrians were grabbed, dragged to the town cross and butchered there. As the spilling of blood upon holy ground was a sin, the abbey had to be reconsecrated.

The pictures of Gloucester were taken between 1891 and 1931. Gloucester was a busy industrial city and inland port, with a skyline dominated by the great pinnacled tower of the cathedral. A former Benedictine abbey founded in 1089, Gloucester Cathedral is where the remains of Edward II were eventually buried following his murder at Berkeley Castle. The cathedral is noted for its great east window, which covers an area of 2700 sq ft and was built to commemorate the victory over the French at Crecy in 1346. Gloucester has been a port since Roman times; the docks flourished following the opening of the Gloucester & Sharpness Canal in 1827. The canal by-passed the hazardous waters of the lower Severn and enabled vessels of up to 190 ft x 29 ft x 10 ft draught to reach the city. The Roman port handled cargoes that included wine from France and Spain, olive oil, pottery, and fish sauce. During the medieval period its principal imports were French wine, pickled herrings, olive oil, and millstones. Gloucester's real claim to fame, however, is that it was here at Christmas 1085 that William the Conqueror ordered the compiling of what has become known to us as the Domesday Book. It had been a bad year for William: troops had been brought in from Normandy and Brittany to reinforce England's defences against an expected invasion by Cnut of Denmark. In some parts of the country the Normans had already laid coastal areas waste so as to deny supplies to Cnut's forces, and William was facing a logistical nightmare. He needed to know what England was worth, what size of army it could support and where, and how much it could pay in taxes. The Domesday survey 'about this land, how it was peopled, and with what sort of men', was to gather information on each estate as it was in the time of Edward the Confessor, its state when the present owner took over, and what it was like in 1086.

Further down river we eventually come to Avonmouth, Clifton and Bristol. Bristol was once the second most important city in England after London; its Mariners' Guild was founded in 1445 and the Fellowship of Merchants in 1500. In 1552 the Merchant Venturers were incorporated; from then on Bristol ships might be found anywhere in the known world. Though most were involved in the trade with Spain, during the grain shortages of the 1580s several ships made trips to the Baltic. Bristol was a port of departure for a number of voyages of exploration and colonisation. From here John Cabot sailed west to reach mainland North America in 1497; Sir Henry Gilbert attempted to settle Newfoundland in 1583; and a similar venture was led by John Guy in 1610. In 1603 Martin Pring had set out to explore New England, and in 1631 Captain Thomas James's expedition to James Bay led to the establishment of the Hudson's Bay Co.

During the Civil War the possession of Bristol was vital to the King's cause. While the Royal Standard flew over the city, diplomatic initiatives to obtain foreign military assistance had currency. If Bristol fell, then the King's cause would be seriously undermined. On 15 March 1643 Sir William Waller, with a force of fewer than 2000 Parliamentary troops, had managed to secure the city, but the following July he was badly defeated at Roundway Down and his army all but destroyed. Prince Rupert marched on Bristol (whose garrison had been stripped by Waller prior to his defeat) and summoned its defenders under Colonel

Nathaniel Fiennes to surrender. Fiennes rejected the offer, and two days later the Royalists attacked. Despite an outstanding defence which inflicted heavy casualties on the Royalists, Fiennes had little hope of holding out, and had no alternative but to ask for terms. Magnanimous in victory, Rupert allowed the garrison to march out of the city with the full honours of war, drums beating and flags flying. Despite his stand, Fiennes was tried the following August and condemned to death, though he was later reprieved. Bristol now became the major Royalist base in the West Country for both land and naval operations, and a port for blockade runners bringing weapons and supplies from Europe. Mindful of Fiennes' experience in defending a city with a large perimeter, Prince Rupert set about strengthening the defences, which included the construction of the Royal Fort on Windmill Hill. Following Marston Moor, Rupert returned to Bristol in October 1644 to organise defences; he prepared for an expected siege, which came the following August after the Royalist disaster at Naseby. Ordering the burning of Clifton, Bedminster and Westbury, Rupert pulled his forces into the city. Though Rupert wrote to the King promising to hold Bristol, his own combat experience must have told him that it was a hopeless case. He put up a stiff resistance, but the parleying for terms began on 4 September 1645; the final surrender occurred on 10 September. With the loss of Bristol, it could be argued that the war was lost.

For a time Bristol dominated the slave trade. Not all the slaves handled by Bristol were from Africa. From the early years of the 17th century, an estimated 50,000 men and women were sentenced by English courts to servitude in the colonies of the New World; the majority were destined to end up working on plantations. It was soon realised, however, that if the plantation system was to be maintained and expanded an alternative source of additional labour had to be found; by 1619 the first cargoes of negro slaves were being landed. Until the Restoration, slaving was carried on by English, Dutch and a few colonial ships, but the majority of merchants

West African coast, slaving at will. And this is precisely what most of them did. Despite a petition from the Royal African Company, Parliament threw the slave trade open to anyone prepared to pay 10 per cent tax on a voyage. In 1707-08, of the 52 ships that cleared Bristol to take part in the Guinea trade, fifty were free traders. In 1725 Bristol cleared 63 ships with a total capacity for 16,950 slaves; though twenty years later the

BRISTOL 1887 20133

involved in the Guinea trade, as it was called, were more interested in gold and ivory than in human cargo. Things changed in the 1660s with the establishment of the joint-stock Royal African Company. From now on, slaving would become the main traffic. The Royal African Company tried to maintain a monopoly on the slave trade, and though a few Bristol merchants held shares in it, most were for free trade; they were of the opinion that any competent captain could cruise the

number of ships had been reduced to 47, the carrying capacity had dropped by only 310 slaves. Though Bristol and London controlled slaving, they were soon to be eclipsed by a new player, Liverpool. With a different pay structure in operation, Liverpool ships were more profitable per voyage than their rivals in London and Bristol. In 1753 Liverpool cleared 63 slavers, Bristol 27, London 13, Lancaster 7, Glasgow 4, Chester 1, and Plymouth 1. Between 1756 and 1786 a total of

588 slaving voyages were made from Bristol, while Liverpool vessels made 1,858.

The last section of the book looks at towns on the west bank of the Severn, including Newnham, Lydney and Chepstow. The pictures of Chepstow include two of the castle, the construction of which was begun by William Fitz Osbern in 1067 as a border fortress. Fitz Osbern chose his site well: a narrow ridge high above the Wye that could be defended on the landward side with a ditch. To the right of the entrance you will see a large D-shaped tower. Known as Marten's Tower, it was erected by Roger Bigod III between 1285 and 1293. It is protected at ground level by two spur bastions from attack by battering ram or undermining. The tower derives its name from Henry Marten (1602-80), who was imprisoned here in fairly comfortable circumstances for twenty years until his death in 1680. Marten was one of the more colourful characters to emerge during the Civil War. He was a signatory to the death warrant of Charles I; the designer of England's Great Seal under the Republic; a rabid republican to the extent that he frightened most Parliamentarians; a wealthy landowner; and a party animal who liked his drink, and women even more. It was his inability to control his finances that landed him in prison for debt; at the Restoration he would almost certainly have faced the death penalty, were it not for the fact that he had some years before fallen out with Cromwell. Marten was convinced that Cromwell really did want to be king, and became an outspoken critic of the Lord Protector and all his works.

This book is not an academic history of the area, but rather a look along the Severn as it was captured on film by our cameramen over a period of eighty years.

CHEPSTOW, HIGH STREET 1906 54507

SHREWSBURY
The English Bridge 1931 83873

Like the city of Durham, Shrewsbury was founded on a
peninsula of high ground almost completely surrounded by
water. As Pengwern, it was a principal stronghold of the Princes
of Powys until the late 8th century, when it fell to the Mercians.

For the next five hundred years or so, Shrewsbury, like
Hereford and Chester, would be an English frontier town; it was
fought for by Welsh patriots, Normans and rebellious barons
alike. It was to Shrewsbury in 1283 that Dafydd ap Gruffydd,
brother of the late Llywelyn, Prince of Wales, was brought
captive from Rhuddlan Castle, to be tried, found guilty, and
hung, drawn and quartered.

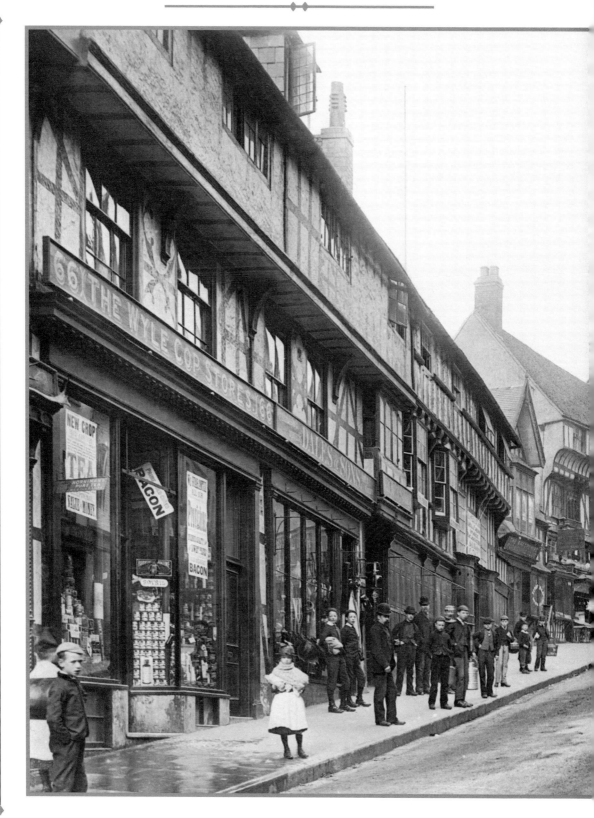

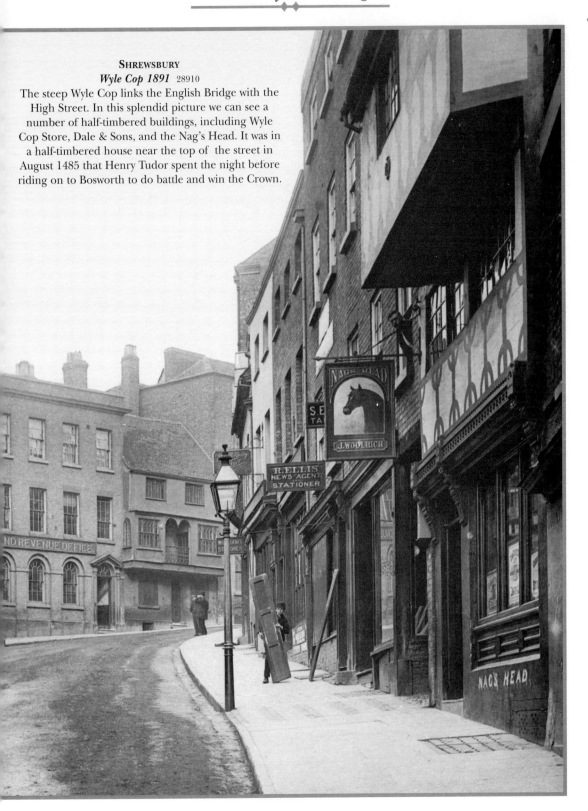

SHREWSBURY
Wyle Cop 1891 28910

The steep Wyle Cop links the English Bridge with the High Street. In this splendid picture we can see a number of half-timbered buildings, including Wyle Cop Store, Dale & Sons, and the Nag's Head. It was in a half-timbered house near the top of the street in August 1485 that Henry Tudor spent the night before riding on to Bosworth to do battle and win the Crown.

SHREWSBURY
The Raven Hotel 1911 63223
Before the Great War, rooms at the Raven were the
most expensive in Shrewsbury, starting from 4s 6d; yet
for some reason now lost to us, dinner here (at 2s 6d)
was the cheapest among the hotels (3s 6d minimum at
the George). Anyway, the Raven is not remembered
for its culinary offerings, but as the place where
Farquhar wrote his play 'The Recruiting Officer'.

SHREWSBURY, HIGH STREET 1931 83877

High street shoppers in 1931 were finding that prices were continuing to fall back to their pre-Great War levels. Between 1914 and 1920 there had been huge increases in the prices of even the most basic of foodstuffs. At the butcher's a pound of streaky bacon had cost 1s 3d in 1914, 2s 7d in 1920, but had fallen back to 1s 7d by 1931. Similarly, a dozen eggs had cost 1s 3d in 1914, 4s 6d in 1920, but again had fallen back to 2s by 1931.

SHREWSBURY, THE BOATHOUSE 1911 63218

The Boat House Inn ferry offered a more sedate way of crossing the Severn than by the nearby Kingsland Bridge.

SHREWSBURY
The River and the School 1923
Ranked as one of the country's top public schools, Shrewsbury was founded as a grammar school by Edward VI in 1552. It moved to its present location on the brow of a hill on the Kingsland side of the river in 1882. Among its old boys were Charles Darwin and Judge Jeffreys.

ATCHAM
The Bridge and the Church 1891
There was a crossing point over the Severn here in Roman times. The seven-arched bridge is made from sandstone.
It was designed by John Gwynne, a founder member of the Royal Academy, and constructed in 1771. Gwynne's other work includes the English Bridge, Shrewsbury (1769) and Magdalen Bridge, Oxford.

SHREWSBURY, THE RIVER AND THE SCHOOL 1923   73818

ATCHAM, THE BRIDGE AND THE CHURCH 1891   28958

ATCHAM, THE CHURCH 1891 28960
Atcham church is dedicated to St Eata. The lower part of the tower is 13th-century, though it uses salvaged Roman stone. There is some 15th-century stained glass acquired second-hand from Bacton, Herefordshire.

BUILDWAS, THE ABBEY 1892 30883
This was a Cistercian abbey founded in 1135 by Roger de Clinton, Bishop of Coventry and Lichfield. This picture shows the remains of the nave, noted for its sturdy-looking round pillars that support a series of Norman arches.

BUILDWAS, THE ABBEY 1896 38115
Despite the trees, this picture gives us an idea of what remains of Buildwas. Despite its great age - the buildings are thought to date from c1150 - it is remarkably well preserved.

BUILDWAS C1955 B244005

Though Buildwas is famed for its ruined abbey, it was here that Thomas Telford's first iron bridge was erected. Telford was a pioneer in the use of iron for structures; though his Buildwas bridge over the Severn no longer exists, other examples of his work still do.

MADELEY, MADELEY COURT 1896 38118

Madeley Court dates from the Tudor period, and was the oldest building in the old village of Madeley (now a part of Telford). It looks as though some work is being done on the roof, and the buildings appear to be intact and free of ivy. In later years part of Madeley Court would become a ruin.

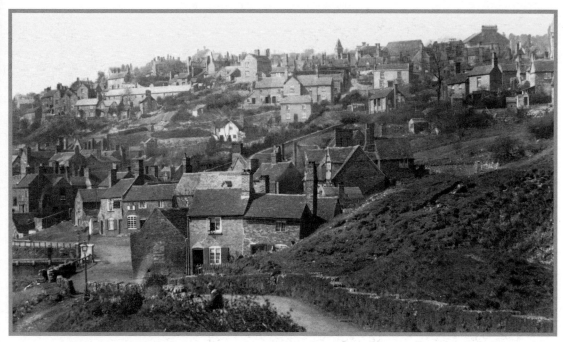

MADELEY, THE VILLAGE 1896 38120A

During the first half of the 19th century, pottery was being produced at Madeley; just a couple of miles to the south was the famous Coalport china works. Nearby Brosley was noted for the manufacture of clay pipes.

IRONBRIDGE, THE BRIDGE 1904 51376

In 1779 Abraham Darby II's Coalbrookdale Ironworks cast the ribs of this, the world's first iron bridge. It is a single-arched structure weighing 380 tons, with a span of 100 ft and an overall length of 196 ft. Today the bridge is restricted to pedestrian traffic only.

IRONBRIDGE 1892 30891

The boat in this picture, probably a shallow draft Severn trow, would have attracted little or no attention from the locals. Not so in 1787. The village was buzzing with excitement as crowds gathered to watch ironmaster John Wilkinson make a fool of himself. He had announced his intention to launch an iron boat onto the Severn near the bridge. Everyone knew iron was heavier than water, so the boat must sink. It didn't.

IRONBRIDGE, FROM THE EAST 1896 38106

It was Abraham Darby's partners, Quaker merchants from Bristol, who put up most of the £3500 needed to establish Coalbrookdale Ironworks. Darby chose the location with care; supplies of coal, iron ore, and water were readily available, and there was access to the Bristol Channel ports by way of the Severn.

IRONBRIDGE, THE TOWN 1925 76923

Here we see the town centre, such as it was, with the municipal buildings in the centre of the picture. The town also has a Market House, which like many others, was originally open on the ground floor.

IRONBRIDGE, FROM THE ROTUNDA 1892 30892

This picture affords us a view across Ironbridge. Here we get an idea of just how steep the limestone slopes are upon which the town is built, and how narrow the gorge is through which the river flows.

IRONBRIDGE, WATERWHEEL 1892 30898

Water power played an important role in the development of the factory system, for it was harnessed to drive machinery in cotton and woollen mills alike. Water was also used for pumping and lifting in mines and for crushing ore, and Abraham Darby used vast amounts of water to work the bellows of his blast furnace at Coalbrookdale.

BRIDGNORTH, THE BRIDGE 1898 42624

BRIDGNORTH
The Bridge 1898
Bridgnorth is really two towns, High Town at the top of a steep hill and Low Town at the bottom. On the extreme left of this picture you can see the Castle Hill Cliff Railway, built to link the towns in 1892. Though only two hundred feet long, the railway rises one hundred feet in height.

BRIDGNORTH
The Cliff Railway c1955
The railway was originally worked by a water-balance system, but this was eventually replaced with colliery winding equipment. The poet and railway buff Sir John Betjeman likened a trip upon the cliff railway to a journey to heaven.

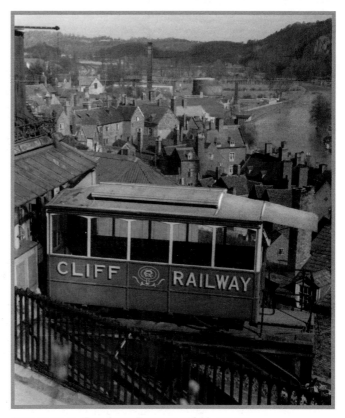

BRIDGNORTH, THE CLIFF RAILWAY c1955 B204064

BRIDGNORTH, THE NORTH GATE 1896 38127

The North Gate is the only part of the town's defences to survive, apart from the remains of the 12th-century castle. Even in the 1580s, the castle was described by John Leland as being 'totally to ruin', but the Parliamentarians finally destroyed the castle in 1646 with gunpowder. Their activities left a section of the keep leaning over at an angle of 17 degrees, three times that of the leaning tower of Pisa. The North Gate itself was heavily restored during the 18th century.

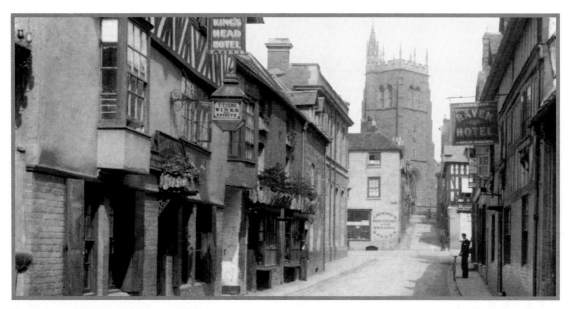

BRIDGNORTH, WHITBURN STREET 1898 42630

By the late 1890s, Bridgnorth was a carpet-making town with a population of about 6000. Even at this date, there were very few buildings around from before the Civil War, as much of the town had been destroyed by fire in 1646. Seen here is the parish church of St Leonard. It too was badly damaged during the Civil War. Constructed of red sandstone, St Leonard's was rebuilt in the 19th century in a 15th-century style. Note the stair turret topped off with its own spire.

BRIDGNORTH, FROM CASTLE WALK 1898 42623
This is a view over Low Town from about one hundred feet above the Severn. The bridge is thought to have been rebuilt by Thomas Telford, who was also responsible for designing the local church dedicated to St Mary Magdalene. St Mary's is unusual in that Telford designed it in a Mediterranean style, with Tuscan columns and a pillared tower topped off with a dome.

UPPER ARLEY, THE LANDING STAGE 1910 62370
The ferry operated between 6.00am and 10.00pm at all times, except at high water. The ferry could take small vehicles, though the approach was difficult and they were carried at their owner's risk.

BEWDLEY, THE RIVER C1938 B82009

Once a thriving port, Bewdley paid the price for turning away the Staffordshire & Worcestershire Canal Co, who wanted to connect with the Severn here. By the end of the 18th century, the Severn north of Bewdley was becoming increasingly difficult to keep open for navigation, and groups of men had to be employed to bow-haul craft between Bewdley and Coalbrookdale. When this practice finally died out, river traffic north of Stourport died with it.

BEWDLEY, WRIBBENHALL C1965 B82071

Wribbenhall is situated on the opposite bank of the river to Bewdley, and architecturally its streets are far more interesting than Severnside. Wribbenhall has a row of early 18th-century terraced cottages, late 18th- and early 19th-century warehouses, and a number of timber-framed houses, the oldest dating back to the 16th century.

BEWDLEY, SEVERNSIDE SOUTH c1965 B82062

By the 1960s, only craft drawing less than 21 ins of water could attempt the river north of Stourport, and even then their passage into Bewdley was blocked by a shoal about one mile south of the town. A once prosperous port had long been reduced to the hiring out of canoes and rowing boats.

BEWDLEY, SEVERNSIDE c1960 B82026

Sir Nicholas Pevsner considered Severnside to be 'as good in its own way as the Brinks, Wisbech'. What Sir Nicholas particularly liked about Severnside was the relationship between the buildings and the river; unobstructed by trees or railings.

BEWDLEY, THE RIVER c1960 B82045

Fishermen try their luck. The Severn has long been a favoured destination of fishermen, especially for salmon and elvers. It is also noted for pike, roach, perch, chub and gudgeon. Further downstream, weir pools have became the haunt for barbel, which were introduced into the river in the 1960s.

BEWDLEY, THE BRIDGE 1904 51976

Thomas Telford's three-arched stone bridge dates from 1798 and cost £9000. The town is said to derive its name from 'beau lieu', or beautiful place. At the beginning of the 20th century, Bewdley's population stood at about 2800.

BEWDLEY
Market Square c1950 B82031
Army surplus meets classic British motor cars. The 1950s saw
some British motor manufacturers tinkering with traditional
designs. In 1955 Armstrong Siddeley produced a long-wheeled
version of their Sapphire limousine; Austin-Healey were content
to fit their 100/4 with a four-speed C-series gearbox; and Morris
turned out a long-wheelbase version of the Oxford. However,
the writing was on the wall: 1955 saw a huge increase in the
number of foreign car imports, up from 4600 in 1954
to over 11,100.

BEWDLEY
Load Street 1931 84690

This is the town's main street from Telford's bridge,
looking towards the mid 18th-century church
designed by E & T Woodward. Even in 1931, things
appeared to be geared heavily towards tourists and
trippers: hotels, inns, cafes, ice cream, Parkes fish and
chip saloon, and perhaps a visit to the
Chocolate Box for a gift.

BEWDLEY, LOAD STREET c1955 B82021
We are looking towards Telford's bridge. Load Street is short but wide. The substantial-looking structure on the right with the Doric pilasters is the Town Hall, completed in 1808. Next to it, and somewhat heavily disguised as the town post office, is a 16th-century timber-framed building.

STOURPORT-ON-SEVERN 1931 84626
The intended junction for the Staffs & Worcs Canal and the River Severn was to have been at Bewdley, but the locals objected. Four miles downstream, where the Stour joined the Severn, stood the sleepy hamlet of Lower Mitton. Soon the place was a hive of activity: basins, warehouses and boatyards were built, and Stourport-on-Severn was born.

STOURPORT-ON-SEVERN C1955 S214022

At Stourport, cargoes were transhipped between Staffs & Worcs narrowboats and Severn trows - these were sailing barges that operated to and from the Bristol Channel ports. Traffic was such that the two original basins of the 1770s were expanded to five. As Stourport thrived, Bewdley faded into insignificance.

STOURPORT-ON-SEVERN C1965 S214070

There was a time when sailing barges could (albeit with difficulty) navigate the Severn as far as Welshpool, 128 miles above Gloucester. Long before this picture was taken, the northern Severn had effectively been closed to navigation at two to three hundred yards above Stourport Bridge.

STOURPORT-ON-SEVERN, THE WEIR c1965 S214036
An excursion craft passes the weir close to Lincomb Lock, now the most northern on the river. This part of the Severn between Stourport and Lenchford remains one of its most pleasant stretches, the river running through a valley and wooded hills.

HOLT FLEET 1907 59103
Our man from Frith manages to capture a picture of the small river steamer that operated between Worcester and Holt Fleet during the summer months. The bridge was designed by Thomas Telford and erected in 1828.

HOLT FLEET, THE WARFE HOTEL c1955 H103055

Holt Fleet in the 1950s was popular and unspoilt; today it is cluttered with caravans. Trippers could take lunch or afternoon tea at the Holt Fleet or the Warfe hotels, and perhaps make a visit to nearby Holt Castle, a 19th-century battlemented country house incorporating parts of a 14th-century fortress.

HOLT FLEET, THE LOCKS c1955 H103059

Holt is 36 miles from Gloucester and six miles from Stourport. Holt Fleet is one of five locks remaining on the Severn; there were others beyond Bewdley, and here the water level changes by five feet. Craft navigating between Worcester and Stourport are allowed maximum dimensions of 90ft length, beam 19ft and headroom 20ft.

HALLOW, ST PETER AND ST JAMES' CHURCH c1960 H152011
This massive-looking church was built between 1867 and 1869 in a 13th-century style to the designs of W J Hopkins. The broach spire was added in 1879. Note the rounded windows in the clerestory.

HALLOW C1960 H152005

Hallow was the home in later years of Sir Charles Bell (1774-1842). He was professor of anatomy and surgery at the Royal College of Surgeons, and pioneered research on the motor and sensory nerves in the brain. He is buried in the local churchyard.

WORCESTER, THE CATHEDRAL 1891 29298

The present cathedral was begun in 1084 as the church of a Benedictine Priory by Wulfstan, Bishop of Worcester since 1062. Wulfstan was a former ally of King Harold, and also his spiritual guide. In 1066 Harold had taken Wulfstan with him when he had travelled north to seek acceptance from the Northumbrians. After Hastings, Wulfstan submitted to William the Conqueror, and was one of the few Saxon Bishops to retain his office.

WORCESTER
The Cross 1899 44010

This view looks along Foregate Street; the bridge carrying the Great Western Railway lines to Hereford and South Wales can be seen in the background. At this date, the town's tramway system was still horse-drawn, and would remain so for another five years. The town" cabs represented good value for money. Shoppers could club together and hire them by the drive: 1s for 1-2 persons, 1s 6d for 3 persons and 2s for 4 persons. Shopping and luggage up to 56lb in weight was carried free of charge; over 56lb it was 1s per cwt.

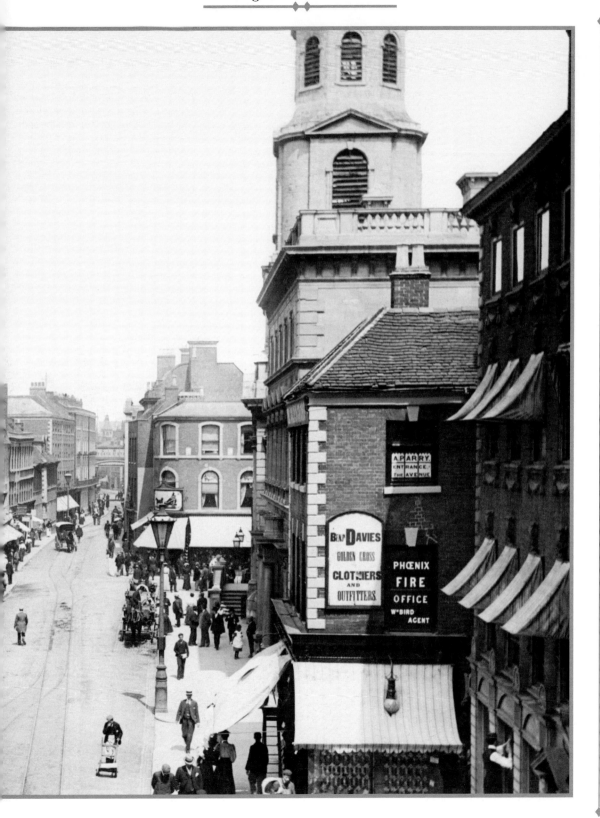

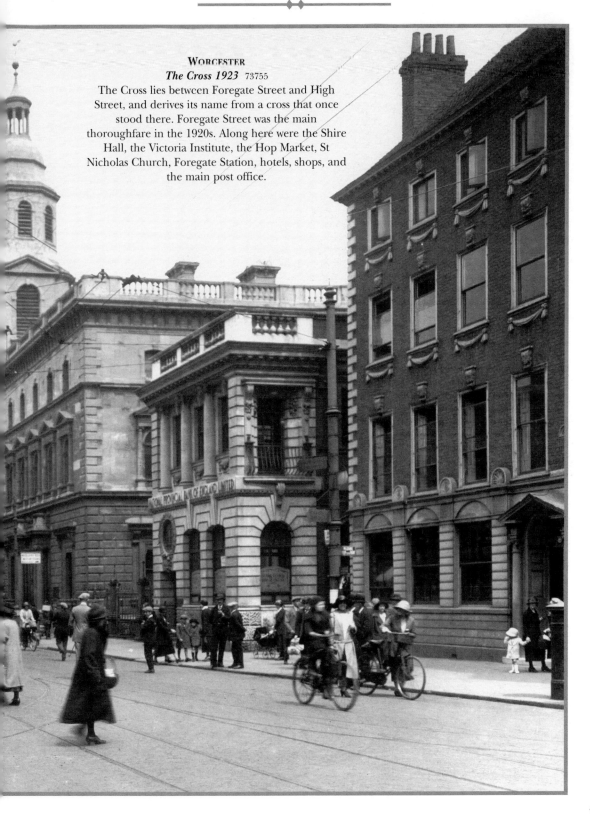

WORCESTER
The Cross 1923 73755
The Cross lies between Foregate Street and High Street, and derives its name from a cross that once stood there. Foregate Street was the main thoroughfare in the 1920s. Along here were the Shire Hall, the Victoria Institute, the Hop Market, St Nicholas Church, Foregate Station, hotels, shops, and the main post office.

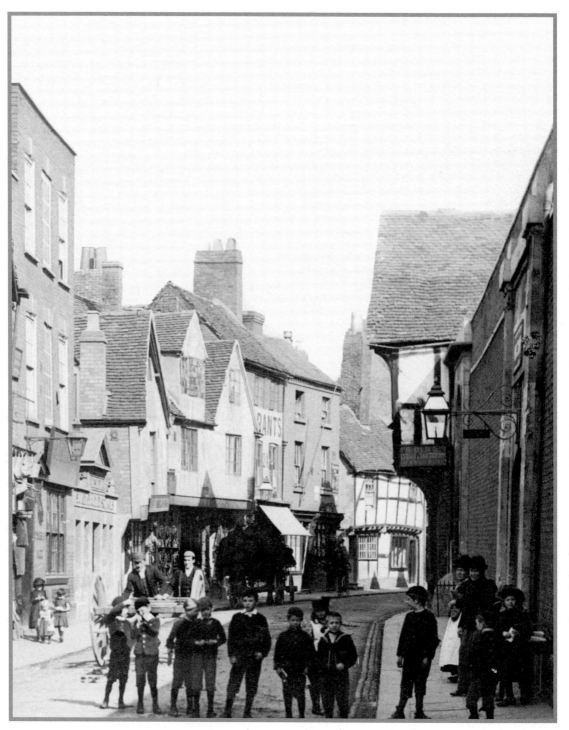

WORCESTER, FRIAR STREET 1891 29321
Friar Street was an odd assortment of buildings, including a number of 15th- and 16th-century half-timbered houses and shops. Though its front dated from 1480, No 32 was where visitors to the Franciscan friary (founded in 1239) lodged. We must be thankful that a number of the buildings in this street have been preserved.

Kempsey, The River and Church 1910 62361
Kempsey lies between Worcester and Severn Stoke. Today there are moorings along the river bank, and housing development has completely swamped the old village.

Kempsey, The River Severn 1910 62364
All is peace and quiet on the banks of the Severn. As a whole, Gloucestershire in 1910 was an agricultural county, with 650,000 acres under cultivation; two-thirds was grasses, and 40,000 given over to wheat. The land supported around 130,000 cattle, 348,000 sheep, and 30,000 horses. However, though the population had doubled between 1801 and 1901, the numbers working on the land, as with the majority of counties, had fallen. There was a significant decrease between 1891 and 1901.

KEMPSEY 1910 62358
A waggonette awaits its passengers prior to setting off for Worcester. These vehicles were extremely popular for short distance excursion work, and were also used to operate scheduled services between towns and outlying villages, especially on market days.

KEMPSEY 1892 29897
This is the old part of the village close to the church. Despite post Second World War development, several thatched cottages have survived to the present day.

KEMPSEY, THE CHURCH 1892 29894
The village church was far larger than the local population could support. This was because the Bishops of Worcester maintained a palace in the village, and the church had to be big enough to accommodate the Bishop's entourage.

UPTON-ON-SEVERN 1931 84660

Upton is situated upon the Severn some ten miles south of Worcester. Apart from vinegar-making, the site of several skirmishes for control of the bridge during the Civil War, and an old church with an oddly-shaped tower, Upton's other claim to fame is that Henry Fielding chose the White Lion in the High Street as one of the settings for his lively novel 'Tom Jones'.

UPTON-ON-SEVERN 1931 84663

During the Civil War, the bridge over the Severn at Upton was of strategic importance to forces investing Worcester. In 1651 Edward Massey, who had held Gloucester for Parliament during the First Civil War, joined King Charles II at Worcester. Realising the threat posed by the bridge, Massey attempted to secure it for the King, but was seriously injured in doing so. The King's forces at Worcester was thereby robbed of its most able field officer.

UPTON-ON-SEVERN, THE BRIDGE 1904 51967

In this picture the old church is still roofed, even though it had been abandoned for over twenty-five years. The tower is 13th-century, but the unusual copper cupola was added in 1769 - it was designed by Anthony Keck. The main body of the church was demolished in the 1930s.

TEWKESBURY, HIGH STREET 1891 29380

Lack of major industrial development in Tewkesbury meant that the town retained much of its 17th- and 18th-century character and did not experience much of an explosion in its population. In 1831, a year the old man on the left of the picture might well have remembered, Tewkesbury's population of just 5780 returned two MPs to Parliament, though this did not beat Old Sarum, whose seven electors also returned two MPs. Bristol, with a population of 150,000, also returned two MPs, but Stroud and Cheltenham were not represented.

TEWKESBURY
Church Street 1907 59071
The town still retains a large number of half-timbered buildings, including several inns, such as the Bell, the Wheatsheaf, Ye Olde Berkeley Arms and the Black Bear. The Black Bear lays claim to being the oldest inn, dating from 1308, while the Bell, though older in that it contains some 13th-century wall paintings, was originally a guest-house for the abbey.

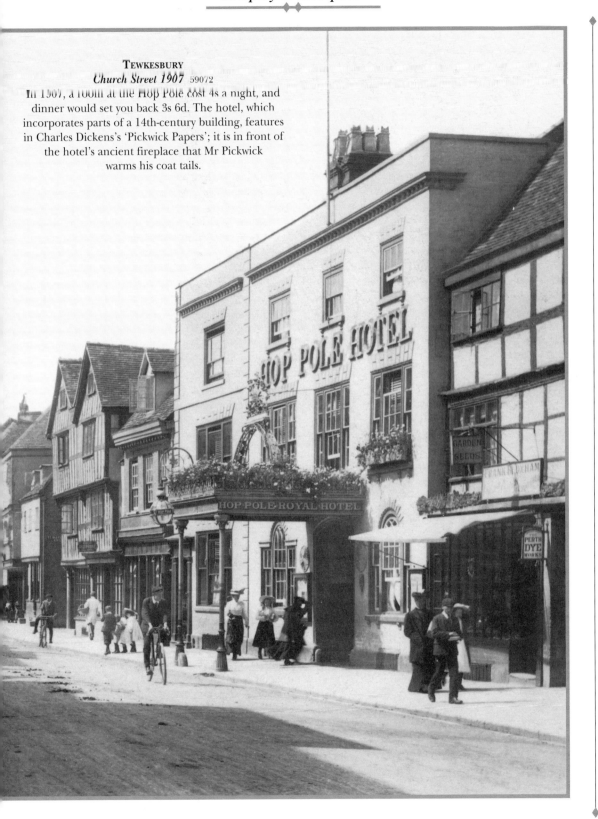

TEWKESBURY
Church Street 1907 59072
In 1907, a room at the Hop Pole cost 4s a night, and dinner would set you back 3s 6d. The hotel, which incorporates parts of a 14th-century building, features in Charles Dickens's 'Pickwick Papers'; it is in front of the hotel's ancient fireplace that Mr Pickwick warms his coat tails.

DEERHURST, THE SAXON CHURCH 1901 47306

St Mary's is one of the finest Saxon churches in Britain. The minster of Deerhurst-on-Severn is known to have existed in the early 9th century, but was later destroyed by Danish raiders. The church was rebuilt in c930, and the nave of the present building is the oldest part still standing. The west tower was originally built as a two-storey porch in c1030, and the aisles were added around the year 1200.

DEERHURST, THE SAXON CHAPEL 1901 47309

Lying two hundred yards south-west of St Mary's the chapel is a small church built by Earl Odda and dedicated to the Holy Trinity in April 1056. It is also thought to be a memorial to Odda's brother Aelfric. The half-timbered building is known as Abbot's Court.

GLOUCESTER, THE DOCKS 1912 65114

For years two small steam packets provided a daily scheduled service between Gloucester and Sharpness, calling at a number of villages and convenient stopping-places along the way. In 1907 the return fare between Gloucester and Sharpness was 1s 9d first class, 1s 3d second class. Fares between some of the intermediate stops could be as low as 2d each way.

GLOUCESTER, THE DOCKS 1923 73689

The 1920s were to bring about something of a mini-boom in the amount of traffic using Gloucester, for it was then that a number of companies, including National Benzole, opened oil terminals at the docks. Other terminals were opened at Sharpness, Worcester and Stourport-on-Severn. Because of the depth of water beyond Sharpness, tankers bound for Gloucester were restricted to a maximum cargo capacity of 750 tons.

GLOUCESTER

Northgate Street 1904 51988

We are looking towards the Cross, where Northgate, Southgate, Eastgate and Westgate all meet. Northgate's most famous building is probably the New Inn, which dates from c1450; it was first built as a house, and it was here that Lady Jane Gray is said to have been proclaimed queen in 1553.

GLOUCESTER, EASTGATE STREET 1931 83828

Judging by the number of cars parked outside, Blinkhorn & Son are having a good day. However, 1931 was a bad year for British motor manufacturers, with a combined output of just 159,000 cars. Motoring was still the preserve of the middle and leisured classes, though a few companies were providing their travellers (reps) with cars. Though new cars were not subject to purchase tax, they were licensed according to RAC horsepower.

GLOUCESTER, SOUTHGATE STREET 1904 51987

One of Gloucester's new electric street tramcars rattles along Southgate Street in hot pursuit of a local horse-drawn omnibus. Next to the Golden Anchor stands the half-timbered house that once belonged to Robert Raikes.

GLOUCESTER
Westgate Street 1891 29004

This view looks towards St Nicholas Church. It was at a house in
Westgate in February 1555 that Bishop John Hooper spent his
last night before being burnt at the stake in St Mary's Square.
Arrested during the persecution of Protestants that followed
Mary Tudor's accession to the throne, Hooper was held in
custody for seventeen months before the law to burn heretics
was passed. Mary was happy to burn men, women and children;
among others who suffered in Gloucestershire were Edward
Horne of Newent, Thomas Drowry, a blind boy of Gloucester,
John Coberley of Cheltenham, and John Piggott
of Little Sodbury.

GLOUCESTER, RAIKES SUNDAY SCHOOL 1923 73687

Robert Raikes (1735-1811) is acknowledged by many to be the founder of the Sunday school movement, having opened the first such establishment in St Catherine Street in 1780. However, Hannah Ball is said to have opened a Sunday school at High Wycombe in 1769.

GLOUCESTER, FROM THE RIVER 1923 73673

The pinnacled central tower of the cathedral dominates the Gloucester skyline. Built of Painswick stone, the 225 ft high tower was completed in 1450. It took nearly one hundred years to build, and replaced an earlier structure.

GLOUCESTER
The Cathedral 1892 29899

The Cathedral was once the Benedictine Abbey of St Peter. Construction began in 1089 on a site where there had been ecclesiastical houses of one sort or another since 681. The abbey (apart from its Lady Chapel) was finished in 1100, though from the early decades of the 14th century a major rebuilding and expansion programme was embarked upon. This was due to substantial revenues generated from pilgrims visiting the shrine of Edward II. Following his murder at Berkeley Castle in 1327, the King's body was refused burial at a number of places before being accepted by the monks of Gloucester. Within a short while, it was claimed that the King's tomb was a place where miracles were happening; this put Gloucester well and truly on the pilgrim trail.

SHARPNESS, THE DOCKS c1955 S502011
From the 1880s to the mid-1930s, Sharpness was the third largest port in the UK for the importing of timber, including pine and spruce from Canada and the Baltic and teak from Burma. At one time, pine baulks, which were fifty to sixty feet in length, were discharged not onto the docks, but into them. They were then chained together and towed by tug to Gloucester.

SHARPNESS, THE DOCKS c1955 S502004
As well as timber, Sharpness handled all manner of grains, linseed, palm kernels, cotton seed, offal grains and ground nuts. From here anything up to a 1000 tons a day was taken by barge to mills along the reaches of the upper Severn. On the right of the picture is the grain silo. It was built in the 1930s, and had a storage capacity of 10,000 tons.

SHARPNESS, THE DOCKS c1955 S502010

In the years following the end of the second world war, John Harker Ltd built several estuarine tankers on the foreshore at Sharpness. One of them might be in the background of this picture. After launching, the vessels were brought into Sharpness for fitting out. In the great days of sail, Sharpness graving dock was always busy, as most vessels calling at the port had their keels scraped before loading.

SHARPNESS, VINDICATRIX CAMP FROM SILO c1955 S502005

The National Sea Training School trained both deck and catering ratings for service with the Merchant Navy. The trainees slept in the barrack-type accommodation seen in this picture.

SHARPNESS, TRAINING SHIP 'VINDICATRIX' c1955 S502018

SHARPNESS
Training Ship 'Vindicatrix' c1955
Tens of thousands of new entrants into the Merchant Navy received their basic training at 'Vindicatrix'. Built in 1883 as the steel sailing ship 'Arranmore', she spent a number of years as a floating seamen's hostel at Gravesend before being towed to Sharpness in August 1939. At Sharpness, she became the headquarters of the National Sea Training School. In 1967 she was declared redundant and towed to Newport, Gwent, for breaking up. Alas, plans to save her came to nothing.

THE RIVER SEVERN
The Railway Bridge c1955
There were only two other bridges on British Railways that were longer than the Severn Bridge: the second Tay (10,711 ft) and the Forth (8296 ft). The Severn carried the railway lines 70 ft above the high water mark, the second Tay 83.5 ft, and the Forth 156 ft. Following the collapse of Sir Thomas Bouch's first Tay Bridge in December 1879, the Severn enjoyed the status of being the country's longest railway bridge until 1887.

THE RIVER SEVERN, THE RAILWAY BRIDGE c1955 B523011

THE RIVER SEVERN
The Railway Bridge c1955 S502006

Constructed of wrought iron and completed in 1879, the Severn
Bridge was the longest tied-arch, bowstring truss bridge on the
British railway network. At 4161 ft in length, it carried not only
the railway but a gas main. On the evening of 25 October 1960 in
dense fog the bridge was struck by the estuarine tankers
'Arkendale H', carrying 400 tons of heavy fuel oil, and 'Wastdale
H', loaded with 350 tons of petrol. Parts of the bridge fell onto
the tankers, the gas main was fractured, and the resulting
explosion brought down yet more debris onto the vessels. The
heat became so intense that it welded the two ships together. Two
complete sections of the bridge were destroyed. The bridge was
eventually dismantled, part of it being sold to Chile for
re-erection as a road bridge. The wrecks of the tankers
can still be seen.

BERKELEY, MARKET PLACE 1904 51750
Berkeley at the beginning of the 20th century was a small town of just over 6200 inhabitants. Visitors could find accommodation at the Berkeley Arms (rooms 3s; dinner 2s 6d), and those fancying a look round the castle could buy admission tickets from the railway station or Miss Smith's stationers in the High Street.

BERKELEY, THE CASTLE C1955 B72033
The earliest castle on the site was built during the reign of William the Conqueror, but the present structure dates from 1156, when work began on the stone shell keep. Edward II was brought here after he had been deposed, and was placed under the protection of the third Baron Berkeley. However, Berkeley was forced to surrender both castle and his royal prisoner into the hands of Thomas Gurney and Lord Maltrevers. On or about 22 September 1327, they put Edward to death using a red-hot poker - the King's agonising screams could be heard throughout the fortress.

AUST FERRY C1966 S264045

This photograph was taken in the year the Severn Bridge carrying the M4 over the river finally opened. That year, the combined output for British car manufacturers was 1,600,000 vehicles, of which the Ford Cortina was the top seller with 127,000 registrations. The Cortina I, in production between 1962 and 1966, cost £639 when it was launched; the Cortina II, which went into production in 1966, cost £669 for the saloon, £724 for the estate.

AUST FERRY 1966 A100004

As the bridge nears completion, the writing is on the wall for regular ferry services on the Severn. Limited capacity, high operating costs, and people lacking the patience to wait for a ferry, combined to put an end to what would have been a pleasant alternative to driving on a motorway.

THE SEVERN BRIDGE C1966 B38005
The bridge opened in 1966, two years after the Forth road bridge. The Severn Bridge is 5240 ft in length, the central span is 3240 ft and the suspension towers are 400 ft high.

AVONMOUTH, THE DOCKS 1901 46494

In 1901, Avonmouth was chosen by Elder & Fyffes as the UK port for their fortnightly service to Port Limon, Costa Rica. In 1895 Elder Dempster had introduced an Avonmouth-Quebec-Montreal summer service, with winter sailings calling at Halifax and St John's, New Brunswick. With larger steamers coming into service, Avonmouth was expanded. In 1902 work began on the King Edward Dock; an 875ft graving dock was added, and an oil tank farm comprising 27 storage tanks was completed in 1911.

AVONMOUTH, THE DOCKS 1901 46493

Avonmouth was used by the Imperial Direct West India Mail Service Co, whose ships sported white hulls and yellow funnels. During 1901 four new cargo liners for the IDWIMS Co entered service at Avonmouth: the 'Port Royal', 'Port Antonio', 'Port Maria' and 'Port Morant'. The vessel seen here might be either the 'Port Royal' or 'Port Antonio', both of which were built by Sir Raylton Dixon & Co, Middlesbrough.

SHIREHAMPTON, THE OLD TOLL HOUSE c1955   S271002

SHIREHAMPTON
The Old Toll House c1955

Roads around Bristol were turnpiked from the 1720s, though many were short stretches and often only seven feet wide. The turnpike did not reach Shirehampton (only five miles from Bristol) until the 1750s.

◆

SHIREHAMPTON
The George Inn c1955

By 1939, boundary changes had resulted in Avonmouth and Shirehampton being incorporated into Bristol. After the Great War, Housing Acts provided local authorities with government funding to build houses, which opened up areas such as the Sea Mills Estate to residential development. Between the wars Bristol built 14,200 houses; private developers built a further 22,000.

SHIREHAMPTON, THE GEORGE INN c1955   S270004

CLIFTON
Leigh Woods 1887

Dredgers are at work. Prior to the 1901 expansion programme at Avonmouth, a number of proposals had been aired for the building of dock and cargo handling facilities along the river from Avonmouth to Bristol. The river would have been widened and deepened, horseshoe bends removed altogether, and much of the character of the Gorge destroyed forever.

◆

CLIFTON
The Suspension Bridge 1887

In 1752 William Vick had left some money towards the eventual bridging of the Gorge. It was not until 1829, however, that a competition for a bridge was advertised. By coincidence, a young engineer by the name of Isambard Kingdom Brunel had been staying in Clifton for his health, spending much of his time sketching in the Gorge. Despite his relative inexperience, Brunel's outline design was accepted.

CLIFTON, LEIGH WOODS 1887   20175

CLIFTON, THE SUSPENSION BRIDGE 1887   20168

CLIFTON, THE SUSPENSION BRIDGE 1887 20163
Brunel estimated that the bridge would cost £52,966 to construct. Brilliant engineer he may have been, but Brunel never would be any good at estimating costs; on more than one occasion he would bring the Great Western Railway close to bankruptcy. By the time Brunel had completed his final design, the estimate had risen to £57,000. Work began in 1836, but stopped in 1843 when the money ran out. The bridge was finally completed in 1864, and even then the suspension chains were bought second-hand.

CLIFTON, THE SUSPENSION BRIDGE 1873 6990
The importance to Bristol of its Floating Harbour can be gauged from this picture, which shows the Avon at low water. The river has been known to have a maximum rise and fall of 37ft.

CLIFTON
The Suspension Bridge c1950

Even the most hurried of visitors to Clifton was recommended to spend a few coppers and walk to the centre of the bridge and admire the view. It was best at high tide, for then the muddy bottom of the Avon would not be on show.

CLIFTON
The Gorge and Tennis Courts c1950

In August 1920, Bristol Corporation obtained an Act to take over the former BP&PR railway line between Sneyd Park Junction and Hotwells. Unlike Bradford, Bristol was not about to embark on running a railway: they simply wanted the trackbed for a new road to Avonmouth, for the Gorge was not wide enough for both.

CLIFTON, THE SUSPENSION BRIDGE c1950   C120189

CLIFTON, THE GORGE AND TENNIS COURTS c1950   B212187

CLIFTON, THE RIVER 1887 20174

On the left bank is the single track Bristol & Portishead Pier & Railway, which opened as a broad gauge line in April 1867 and was worked by the Bristol & Exeter Railway. On the right bank is the line belonging to the secretive Bristol Port & Pier Railway running between Hotwells and Avonmouth. So secretive were they, that they kept everyone in the dark as to opening day for fear they would be inundated with passengers; they only had one engine. The BP&PR was totally isolated from other railways, for no provision was made for a connection.

CLIFTON C1960 B212312

Clifton became a fashionable spa in the 18th century, and for a time even rivalled Bath. With its new-found status came the trappings: pump room, assembly rooms, even London retailers - who opened for the season, took the money and ran. The well was finally closed after it became contaminated with river water.

CLIFTON, THE ROCKS 1896 38167
The trams of the Bristol Tramways & Carriage Co linked Clifton to the city by way of Hotwells Road. The spa could also be reached from Avonmouth by the trains of the BP&PR, whose terminus can be seen on the extreme left of the picture.

CLIFTON, THE BRIDGE 1887 20167
A paddle-tug awaits its next assignment. During the 1870s and 1880s large numbers of double-engined disconnecting paddle-tugs were built. Each paddle had its own engine, and could be operated independently, thereby giving the tugs great manoeuvrability. However, they lacked the power of screw tugs, and were heavy on operating costs outside the coal handling ports where fuel was relatively inexpensive. The last paddle-tug on the Avon was withdrawn in 1907.

CLIFTON, THE BRIDGE 1900 45555

A screw tug prepares to assist a steamer to its berth in the Floating Harbour. As well as tugs, other service vessels included dredgers and lighters. Of the latter were the 'Garth', 'Maesteg', 'Rhymney' and 'Rhondda'; they were of between 156 and 170 gross tons and belonged to the Bristol Lighterage Co (a subsidiary of Elder Dempster). These small vessels undertook lighterage between Bristol and Avonmouth for Elders ships.

BRISTOL, ENTRANCE TO THE FLOATING HARBOUR c1950 B212186

The Floating Harbour was created in the early years of the 19th century to give Bristol a tide-free dock. It was a remarkable piece of civil engineering, five years in the making and with a cast of several thousand. The project cost about £600,000, and involved diverting the Avon to the south from Totterdown and round the city to link up with its old course. Much of the shovelling was done by French prisoners of war.

BRISTOL, FROM THE GRANARY 1901 47880

We are looking out across the deal and timber yards to the cathedral and downtown Bristol. Perched high on its hill in the background at left is the tower erected to commemorate John Cabot's voyage. Financed by Richard Amerycke, Cabot and his son Sebastian sailed from Bristol on a local ship, the 'Matthew'. On 24 June 1497 they reached the mainland of North America.

BRISTOL, THE DOCKS C1950 B212222

The coaster 'Depa' eases her way into the city dock with a cargo of timber. Other traffic handled here included cargoes from Ireland: steamers from Cork and Waterford discharged cattle into the pens on the foreign animals wharf at Merchants' Dock.

BRISTOL
The Quay 1887 20133

This photograph was taken three years after the city docks, Avonmouth, and Portishead were brought together under Corporation control. This meant that once again Bristol could compete for trade; throughout much of the 19th century it had lost business owing to high dock charges levied by the money-grabbing dock company. At one time, it had been cheaper to land Bristol-bound cargoes at Liverpool and send them on by train than to discharge them on Bristol Quay.

BRISTOL, THE DOCKS c1950 B212217

Bristol developed to become a major centre for the importation of timber for use throughout the west of England. In 1870 the port handled 105,000 tons, and by 1900 it was dealing with over 170,000 tons a year. During the same period, annual tobacco imports through the docks rose from 349 tons in 1880 to 2278 in 1910, and by the mid 1920s the average was 24,000 tons a year. The bumper year for the weed was 1947, with 50,098 tons landed.

BRISTOL, THE DOCKS c1950 B212220

We are looking towards St Augustine's Reach with its long association with Bristol's maritime past. The Reach dates from 1248; when it was first built it extended further into the city. For the mid 13th century, it represented a major feat of civil engineering that involved diverting the course of the River Frome from its ancient junction with the Avon. The Reach established Bristol as a major port.

BRISTOL, THE DOCKS C1950 B212181

The 285ft high spire of St Mary Redcliffe towers above the city docks. This huge parish church, the size of a cathedral, owes much to the generosity of Bristol's merchants, such as William Canynge (who died in 1396) and his grandson William Canynge the younger (1394?-1274).

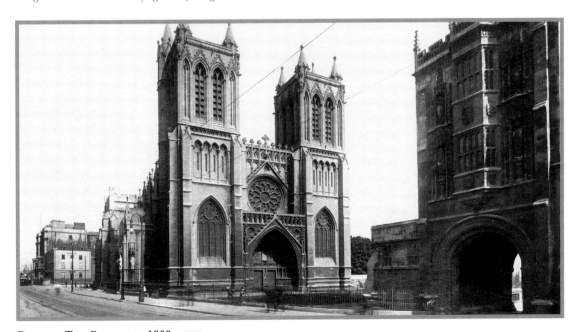

BRISTOL, THE CATHEDRAL 1900 45568

In 1542 Henry VIII created the diocese of Bristol, and the former church of the Augustinian priory was elevated to the rank of cathedral. The building underwent considerable restoration and remodelling between 1868 and 1888, including the construction of the nave and the west towers. Older parts include the Elder Lady Chapel (1210-1215) and the choir (1298-1363).

BRISTOL
Park Street 1900 45653

Here we see Park Street in the days of horse-drawn transport. Half-way up the street is what appears to be a water-cart on damping-down duty. With several thousand animals on the streets every day, the stench from horse-droppings was horrendous, especially during the summer months. Bristol Health Authority was the first to conduct experiments using water-carts. They found that it took 7000 gallons of water to damp down one mile of street 18 ft in width.

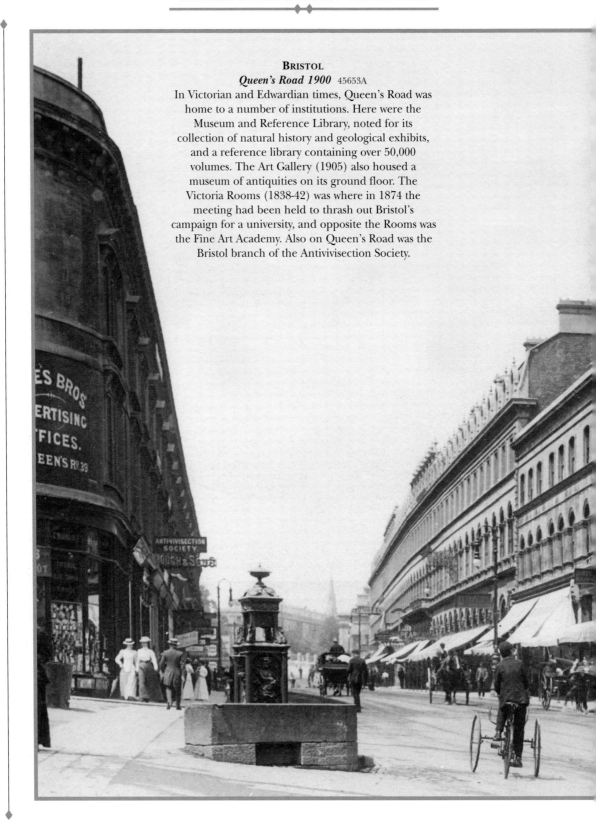

BRISTOL
Queen's Road 1900 45653A

In Victorian and Edwardian times, Queen's Road was home to a number of institutions. Here were the Museum and Reference Library, noted for its collection of natural history and geological exhibits, and a reference library containing over 50,000 volumes. The Art Gallery (1905) also housed a museum of antiquities on its ground floor. The Victoria Rooms (1838-42) was where in 1874 the meeting had been held to thrash out Bristol's campaign for a university, and opposite the Rooms was the Fine Art Academy. Also on Queen's Road was the Bristol branch of the Antivivisection Society.

BRISTOL
St Augustine's Bridge 1901 47885
Car No 118 of the Bristol Tramways &
Carriage Co heads for St Augustine's
Bridge. The tramway was electrified in
1895, but as the Corporation had a legal
right to acquire it in 1915 at book price,
or at any seventh year thereafter, the
company were none too keen to spend
money on improvements. The tramway
creaked on virtually unaltered since the
day it opened, only to be put out of its
misery by the Luftwaffe in 1941.

BRISTOL, KING STREET c1950 B212211
King Street escaped total destruction during the Blitz, though some buildings, such as the Merchant Adventurers'
Almshouses (1699), were damaged. In the 1950s the street retained a number of 17th- and 18th-century properties
such as those seen here.

BRISTOL, THE THEATRE ROYAL 1890 24640
One of the oldest theatres in the country still in regular use, the Theatre Royal dates back to 1766. Its design was
based upon Sir Christopher Wren's Drury Lane Theatre, London, but even when built the Royal had a semi-
circular auditorium. The facade was remodelled during the 19th century.

BRISTOL, PARK STREET 1900 45654

BRISTOL
Park Street 1900
This is Park Street in the days before the top end was dominated by the Gothic tower of the university, designed by Sir George Oatley.

◆

PORTISHEAD
The Pier Approach 1908
Portishead was connected to Bristol by rail in 1867. The following year the pier was commissioned; it was soon extended so that vessels could use it at low water. From here there was an all-year-round steamer service to Cardiff and Newport and summer excursions.

PORTISHEAD, THE PIER APPROACH 1908 75998

PORTISHEAD, THE BEACH 1887 20188

The opening of the railway put Portishead at less than one hour's travelling time from the centre of Bristol. As a result, the little resort became an attractive proposition for Bristol's professional and business people wanting a villa by the sea.

PORTISHEAD, THE ESPLANADE 1924 76002

This was a popular place for trippers, with train services from Temple Meads beginning at 7.00am. On Saturdays the rush to the seaside was catered for at Temple Meads with additional trains at 12.00 noon and 12.57pm, and an extra one from Bedminster at 2.04pm. As no-one was supposed to enjoy their Sundays off, the first train for Portishead did not run until 10.15am; the last one back to Bristol was at 9.48pm.

CLEVEDON, THE PIER 1892 31251

In late Victorian tour guides, Clevedon was noted for its good beach, its pier, and the surrounding countryside, which was considered to be exceptionally beautiful. At only five miles from Portishead, thirteen miles from Bristol and fifteen miles from Weston-super-Mare, Clevedon was well placed to attract day trippers.

CLEVEDON, THE PIER AND THE ROYAL PIER HOTEL c1965 C116048

Clevedon's status as a resort was confirmed in 1869 with the opening of the pier. In later years, well-to-do visitors stayed at the Walton Park Hotel, where rooms were 4s 6d. and dinner 5s a head, whilst those on a health trip could experience various water tortures on offer at the Hydropathic for 7s 6d a day; treatments extra. The Royal Pier was good value at 7s 6d a day all in.

CLEVEDON, GREEN BEACH 1892 31252

By 1892, cycling had become a popular pastime thanks to the introduction of the Safety bicycle. Introduced in 1884, the first Safeties had equal-sized wheels and solid tyres, the latter causing serious vibration problems. However, in 1888 Dunlop brought out their pneumatic tyre, and the cycling craze was on; hotels and inns were soon displaying signs saying 'cyclists welcome'.

CLEVEDON, MARINE PARADE 1913 65397

Clevedon was where Samuel Taylor Coleridge and Sara Fricker spent their honeymoon in 1795. They stayed for two months, not unusually long by honeymoon standards of the day for those who had wealth or position; Sir Charles Monck and his bride honeymooned for two years. In the 1790s, Coleridge was a radical journalist and romantic poet, and his opium addiction lay somewhere in the future.

CLEVEDON, THE CHURCH 1935 86829
St Andrew's Church sits on an unspoilt headland to the south-west of Clevedon. Buried here is Arthur Hallam (1811-1833), the son of historian Henry Hallam (1777-1859). It was Arthur's death that inspired Alfred Lord Tennyson to write his 'In Memoriam'.

CLEVEDON, WALTON CASTLE 1887 20121
Walton Castle stands to the north-east of Clevedon in the middle of what is now a golf course. Despite its looks, Walton was never a fortress; it is an early example of a folly, 'a useless and needlessly extravagant structure', though many have argued that follies are not useless if they give pleasure and arouse interest. Explorers of follies should take extreme care: though many are maintained, others have been neglected, and are dangerous with crumbling walls, rotten timbers etc.

NEWNHAM
High Street c1955 N87011
During the Civil War, Newnham, like many Royalist garrisons
surrounding Gloucester, was on the receiving end of a raid mounted by
Colonel Edward Massey's forces. On 8 May 1644 the Parliamentarians
struck. The Royalists appear to have fortified the church and the area of
the green, but quickly withdrew to the former. They appear to have
been on the point of surrendering when one of them, said to be a
servant of Sir John Winter, put a match to a barrel of gunpowder. The
explosion blew both men and windows out of the church, though there
were no deaths. For whatever reason, the explosion appears to have
unnerved Massey's troops, who then set about butchering the hapless
Parliamentarians, killing about twenty of them before order was at last
restored. The survivors were given quarter. All, that is, except a Captain
Butler, who, being Irish, and therefore a rebel, was killed out of hand.

NEWNHAM, THE UNLAWATER HOTEL C1955 N87020
The hotel dates from the 18th century, though it does incorporate some details from an earlier house on the site. It is noted for its Queen Anne panelling and Ionic columns.

NEWNHAM, THE CLOCK TOWER C1955 N87047
The clock tower dates from 1875, by which time Newnham had long ceased to be the most important Gloucestershire town on the west bank of the river. Until the railways took over long-distance travel, Newnham was a coaching town on the routes to and from the west.

NEWNHAM
The River Severn from the Church c1955

Mothers and daughters take advantage of the excellent views of the Severn afforded them from the churchyard of St Peter's. A church is known to have existed at Newnham in 1080, but it was relocated to its present site by 1380 to avoid flooding; some of the stone was salvaged and used in the rebuilding.

◆

NEWNHAM

For centuries the Severn has been notorious for flooding during the winter months, and much of the lower-lying land is protected with flood defences. In the 14th century Newnham's church suffered sufficient damage for the decision to be taken to relocate it to higher ground.

NEWNHAM, THE RIVER SEVERN FROM THE CHURCH c1955 N87027

NEWNHAM N87006

BLAKENEY c1955 B523004

There are several interesting buildings around Blakeney. At Brain's Farm there is the 16th-century stone-built Hewler's Farmhouse. In Blakeney itself stands Swan House, built as an inn in the 17th century, and the 18th-century King's Head Inn.

BLAKENEY c1955 B523033

All Saints, with its somewhat minimalist battlemented tower, is a c1820 rebuild by Samuel Hewlett of an early 18th-century church. All underwent restoration in 1907.

LYDNEY C1960 L200039

Lydney is situated upon the northern side of the Severn almost opposite Sharpness. The Lydney Canal is just one mile long with one lock and the tidal doors seen here, but it was an important and busy port for the shipment of coal from mines in the Forest of Dean.

LYDNEY, THE DOCKS C1960 L200035

Even in the late 18th century there were ninety pits in the Forest, with a combined annual output of about 100,000 tons of coal. By the 1860s annual output had risen to about 500,000 tons, though 350,000 tons of this was being mined at ten large collieries. At the beginning of the 20th century the combined output of all Gloucestershire pits was about 1.5 million tons.

LYDNEY
High Street c1955 L.200012
It is hard to believe that Lydney's streets once echoed to the
sounds of battle. In early 1644, after nearly three months of
inactivity due to a lack of money, supplies and equipment,
Colonel Edward Massey, the resourceful Parliamentarian
Governor of Gloucester, felt strong enough to mount a series of
raids against the surrounding Royalist garrisons. One such
attack was made against Lydney, where Sir John Winter, Royalist
commander in the Forest of Dean, lived in the heavily
fortified White House.

LYDNEY C1960 L200036

Timber barges from Avonmouth Docks await discharge on the Lydney Canal. The Lydney was once connected to Pidcock's Canal, itself less than two miles in length, which ran to Middle Forge.

LYDNEY, NEWERNE STREET C1950 L200008

This is down-town Lydney in the days when books could be loaned from the newsagents for a few coppers a week via the Argosy Lending Library, and a liquid night out at the Fleece could be had for less than ten bob with enough change for fish and chips on the way home.

LYDNEY
The Cross c1955
Lydney's 14th-century cross was restored in 1878. The parish church also underwent some late 19th-century restoration and remodelling, which included adding a spire to its 13th-century tower.

LYDNEY
Forest Road c1955
The Forest of Dean was an extensive royal hunting ground between the Wye and the Severn, extending as far north as Ross and Gloucester.

LYDNEY, THE CROSS c1955 L200014A

LYDNEY, FOREST ROAD c1955 L200007

CHEPSTOW, THE RIVER SEVERN FERRY 1936 87417

The 'Severn King' at Chepstow landing stage. There was a time when barges could leave the Severn and sail 97 miles up the Wye as for as Hay, but by 1870 navigation was limited to the lower 37 miles. Today the Wye is navigable only as far as Tintern, and even then only at high water.

CHEPSTOW, TOWN GATE 1936 87413

Until the late 13th century, the town of Chepstow appears to have had no defences on its landward side. It was then that Roger Bigod III built the town wall, which was some 1200 yds in length and had a number of semi-circular towers. The only entrance into the town from the west was by way of the town gate.

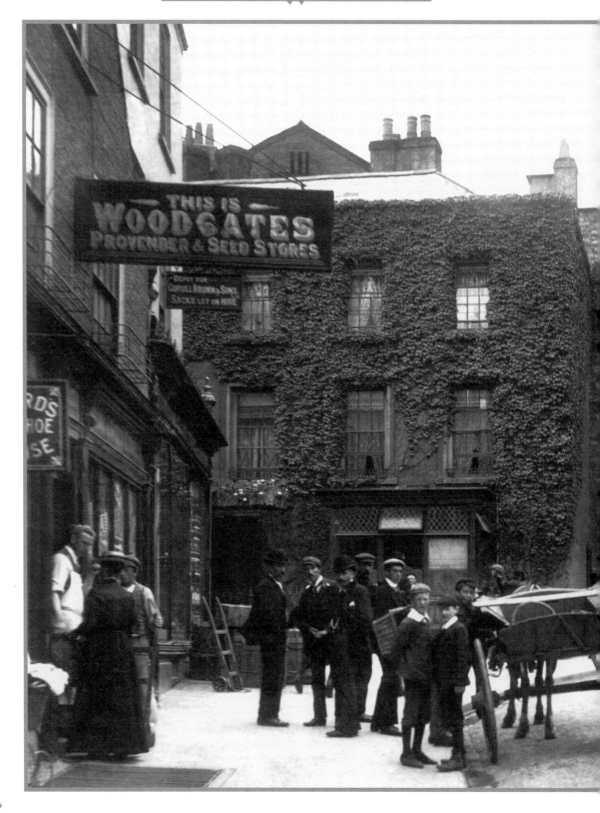

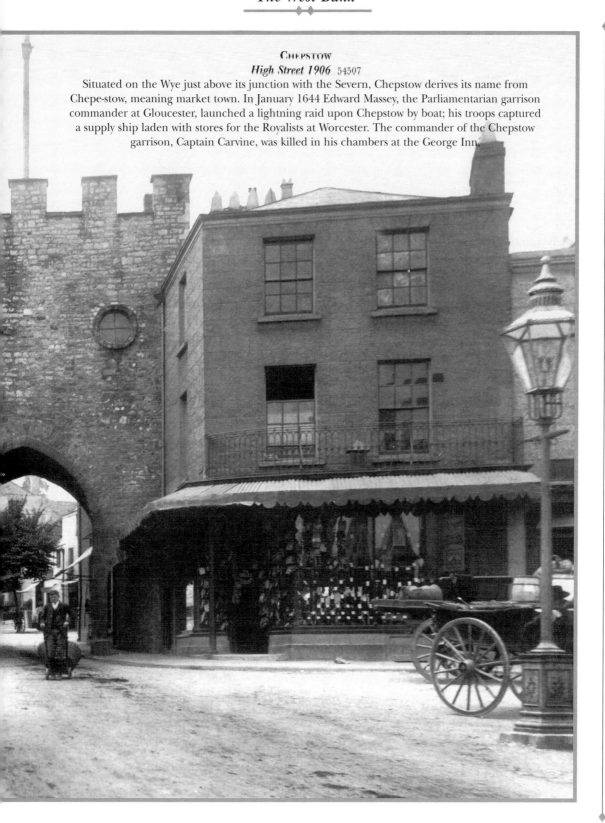

CHEPSTOW
High Street 1906 54507

Situated on the Wye just above its junction with the Severn, Chepstow derives its name from
Chepe-stow, meaning market town. In January 1644 Edward Massey, the Parliamentarian garrison
commander at Gloucester, launched a lightning raid upon Chepstow by boat; his troops captured
a supply ship laden with stores for the Royalists at Worcester. The commander of the Chepstow
garrison, Captain Carvine, was killed in his chambers at the George Inn.

CHEPSTOW
The Castle 1893 32495

In this picture we can see the remains of the two-storey rectangular
fortified hall built by Fitz Osbern on the narrowest part of the ridge.
It is not a keep, as its walls are only 3-6ft thick. On the left is the huge
D-shaped tower built in the late 13th century by Roger Bigod III. It is
protected against attack by battering ram or by undermining with
spur bastions. To the right of it is the twin-towered gatehouse, which
dates from between 1219 and 1245. Originally there would only have
been arrowslits in its front face; the windows are from a later period.
On the top of the gatehouse there would once have been a hourd, or
wooden gallery, from which the castle's archers could command the
ground on the approach to the gate.

CHEPSTOW, THE CASTLE 1893 32493

Chepstow Castle was begun in 1067 by William Fitz Osbern, Lord of Breteuil. At that time Norman expansion into Wales was slow, possibly deliberately so. Norman control over England was effectively limited to the south-east of the country; there were rumours that the sons of King Harold were in contact with King Diarmait of Leinster, who was prepared to provide them with ships and troops to mount an invasion. The Conqueror himself was away in Normandy. Fitz Osbern chose his site for Chepstow Castle well. It sits on a long narrow ridge high above the Wye, its defensive capabilities to landward being enhanced by a ditch.

CHEPSTOW, THE RACES 1938 88687

Bookies and punters alike watch as the second race on the card draws to a close. Judging from the discarded betting slips, the punters had not backed Harry Wragg to get the better of Gordon Richards in the first race.

THE SEVERN BORE 1906 55850A

Twice a year, in April and September, people come from all over to watch the Severn Bore, a wave varying in size from nothing more than a ripple to a wall of water several feet high. The bore occurs when the difference between high and low water is at its greatest, often over thirty feet. The sudden inward rush of water up the Severn is at its best when backed by a south-westerly wind; then the bore is like the one pictured here.

THE SEVERN BORE 1906 55850

Here we see the rolling sea effect of a good-sized Severn Bore. The bore can pose a serious threat to small river craft, but these days it also offers opportunities not to be missed for surfers, waterskiers and canoeists.

Index

Frith Book Co Titles

www.francisfrith.co.uk

The Frith Book Company publishes over 100 new titles each year. A selection of those currently available are listed below. For latest catalogue please contact Frith Book Co.

Town Books 96 pages, approx 100 photos. County and Themed Books 128 pages, approx 150 photos (unless specified). All titles hardback laminated case and jacket except those indicated pb (paperback)

Amersham, Chesham & Rickmansworth (pb)			Derby (pb)	1-85937-367-4	£9.99
	1-85937-340-2	£9.99	Derbyshire (pb)	1-85937-196-5	£9.99
Ancient Monuments & Stone Circles	1-85937-143-4	£17.99	Devon (pb)	1-85937-297-x	£9.99
Aylesbury (pb)	1-85937-227-9	£9.99	Dorset (pb)	1-85937-269-4	£9.99
Bakewell	1-85937-113-2	£12.99	Dorset Churches	1-85937-172-8	£17.99
Barnstaple (pb)	1-85937-300-3	£9.99	Dorset Coast (pb)	1-85937-299-6	£9.99
Bath (pb)	1-85937419-0	£9.99	Dorset Living Memories	1-85937-210-4	£14.99
Bedford (pb)	1-85937-205-8	£9.99	Down the Severn	1-85937-118-3	£14.99
Berkshire (pb)	1-85937-191-4	£9.99	Down the Thames (pb)	1-85937-278-3	£9.99
Berkshire Churches	1-85937-170-1	£17.99	Down the Trent	1-85937-311-9	£14.99
Blackpool (pb)	1-85937-382-8	£9.99	Dublin (pb)	1-85937-231-7	£9.99
Bognor Regis (pb)	1-85937-431-x	£9.99	East Anglia (pb)	1-85937-265-1	£9.99
Bournemouth	1-85937-067-5	£12.99	East London	1-85937-080-2	£14.99
Bradford (pb)	1-85937-204-x	£9.99	East Sussex	1-85937-130-2	£14.99
Brighton & Hove(pb)	1-85937-192-2	£8.99	Eastbourne	1-85937-061-6	£12.99
Bristol (pb)	1-85937-264-3	£9.99	Edinburgh (pb)	1-85937-193-0	£8.99
British Life A Century Ago (pb)	1-85937-213-9	£9.99	England in the 1880s	1-85937-331-3	£17.99
Buckinghamshire (pb)	1-85937-200-7	£9.99	English Castles (pb)	1-85937-434-4	£9.99
Camberley (pb)	1-85937-222-8	£9.99	English Country Houses	1-85937-161-2	£17.99
Cambridge (pb)	1-85937-422-0	£9.99	Essex (pb)	1-85937-270-8	£9.99
Cambridgeshire (pb)	1-85937-420-4	£9.99	Exeter	1-85937-126-4	£12.99
Canals & Waterways (pb)	1-85937-291-0	£9.99	Exmoor	1-85937-132-9	£14.99
Canterbury Cathedral (pb)	1-85937-179-5	£9.99	Falmouth	1-85937-066-7	£12.99
Cardiff (pb)	1-85937-093-4	£9.99	Folkestone (pb)	1-85937-124-8	£9.99
Carmarthenshire	1-85937-216-3	£14.99	Glasgow (pb)	1-85937-190-6	£9.99
Chelmsford (pb)	1-85937-310-0	£9.99	Gloucestershire	1-85937-102-7	£14.99
Cheltenham (pb)	1-85937-095-0	£9.99	Great Yarmouth (pb)	1-85937-426-3	£9.99
Cheshire (pb)	1-85937-271-6	£9.99	Greater Manchester (pb)	1-85937-266-x	£9.99
Chester	1-85937-090-x	£12.99	Guildford (pb)	1-85937-410-7	£9.99
Chesterfield	1-85937-378-x	£9.99	Hampshire (pb)	1-85937-279-1	£9.99
Chichester (pb)	1-85937-228-7	£9.99	Hampshire Churches (pb)	1-85937-207-4	£9.99
Colchester (pb)	1-85937-188-4	£8.99	Harrogate	1-85937-423-9	£9.99
Cornish Coast	1-85937-163-9	£14.99	Hastings & Bexhill (pb)	1-85937-131-0	£9.99
Cornwall (pb)	1-85937-229-5	£9.99	Heart of Lancashire (pb)	1-85937-197-3	£9.99
Cornwall Living Memories	1-85937-248-1	£14.99	Helston (pb)	1-85937-214-7	£9.99
Cotswolds (pb)	1-85937-230-9	£9.99	Hereford (pb)	1-85937-175-2	£9.99
Cotswolds Living Memories	1-85937-255-4	£14.99	Herefordshire	1-85937-174-4	£14.99
County Durham	1-85937-123-x	£14.99	Hertfordshire (pb)	1-85937-247-3	£9.99
Croydon Living Memories	1-85937-162-0	£9.99	Horsham (pb)	1-85937-432-8	£9.99
Cumbria	1-85937-101-9	£14.99	Humberside	1-85937-215-5	£14.99
Dartmoor	1-85937-145-0	£14.99	Hythe, Romney Marsh & Ashford	1-85937-256-2	£9.99

Available from your local bookshop or from the publisher

Frith Book Co Titles (continued)

Ipswich (pb)	1-85937-424-7	£9.99	St Ives (pb)	1-85937415-8	£9.99
Ireland (pb)	1-85937-181-7	£9.99	Scotland (pb)	1-85937-182-5	£9.99
Isle of Man (pb)	1-85937-268-6	£9.99	Scottish Castles (pb)	1-85937-323-2	£9.99
Isles of Scilly	1-85937-136-1	£14.99	Sevenoaks & Tunbridge	1-85937-057-8	£12.99
Isle of Wight (pb)	1-85937-429-8	£9.99	Sheffield, South Yorks (pb)	1-85937-267-8	£9.99
Isle of Wight Living Memories	1-85937-304-6	£14.99	Shrewsbury (pb)	1-85937-325-9	£9.99
Kent (pb)	1-85937-189-2	£9.99	Shropshire (pb)	1-85937-326-7	£9.99
Kent Living Memories	1-85937-125-6	£14.99	Somerset	1-85937-153-1	£14.99
Lake District (pb)	1-85937-275-9	£9.99	South Devon Coast	1-85937-107-8	£14.99
Lancaster, Morecambe & Heysham (pb)	1-85937-233-3	£9.99	South Devon Living Memories	1-85937-168-x	£14.99
Leeds (pb)	1-85937-202-3	£9.99	South Hams	1-85937-220-1	£14.99
Leicester	1-85937-073-x	£12.99	Southampton (pb)	1-85937-427-1	£9.99
Leicestershire (pb)	1-85937-185-x	£9.99	Southport (pb)	1-85937-425-5	£9.99
Lincolnshire (pb)	1-85937-433-6	£9.99	Staffordshire	1-85937-047-0	£12.99
Liverpool & Merseyside (pb)	1-85937-234-1	£9.99	Stratford upon Avon	1-85937-098-5	£12.99
London (pb)	1-85937-183-3	£9.99	Suffolk (pb)	1-85937-221-x	£9.99
Ludlow (pb)	1-85937-176-0	£9.99	Suffolk Coast	1-85937-259-7	£14.99
Luton (pb)	1-85937-235-x	£9.99	Surrey (pb)	1-85937-240-6	£9.99
Maidstone	1-85937-056-x	£14.99	Sussex (pb)	1-85937-184-1	£9.99
Manchester (pb)	1-85937-198-1	£9.99	Swansea (pb)	1-85937-167-1	£9.99
Middlesex	1-85937-158-2	£14.99	Tees Valley & Cleveland	1-85937-211-2	£14.99
New Forest	1-85937-128-0	£14.99	Thanet (pb)	1-85937-116-7	£9.99
Newark (pb)	1-85937-366-6	£9.99	Tiverton (pb)	1-85937-178-7	£9.99
Newport, Wales (pb)	1-85937-258-9	£9.99	Torbay	1-85937-063-2	£12.99
Newquay (pb)	1-85937-421-2	£9.99	Truro	1-85937-147-7	£12.99
Norfolk (pb)	1-85937-195-7	£9.99	Victorian and Edwardian Cornwall	1-85937-252-x	£14.99
Norfolk Living Memories	1-85937-217-1	£14.99	Victorian & Edwardian Devon	1-85937-253-8	£14.99
Northamptonshire	1-85937-150-7	£14.99	Victorian & Edwardian Kent	1-85937-149-3	£14.99
Northumberland Tyne & Wear (pb)	1-85937-281-3	£9.99	Vic & Ed Maritime Album	1-85937-144-2	£17.99
North Devon Coast	1-85937-146-9	£14.99	Victorian and Edwardian Sussex	1-85937-157-4	£14.99
North Devon Living Memories	1-85937-261-9	£14.99	Victorian & Edwardian Yorkshire	1-85937-154-x	£14.99
North London	1-85937-206-6	£14.99	Victorian Seaside	1-85937-159-0	£17.99
North Wales (pb)	1-85937-298-8	£9.99	Villages of Devon (pb)	1-85937-293-7	£9.99
North Yorkshire (pb)	1-85937-236-8	£9.99	Villages of Kent (pb)	1-85937-294-5	£9.99
Norwich (pb)	1-85937-194-9	£8.99	Villages of Sussex (pb)	1-85937-295-3	£9.99
Nottingham (pb)	1-85937-324-0	£9.99	Warwickshire (pb)	1-85937-203-1	£9.99
Nottinghamshire (pb)	1-85937-187-6	£9.99	Welsh Castles (pb)	1-85937-322-4	£9.99
Oxford (pb)	1-85937-411-5	£9.99	West Midlands (pb)	1-85937-289-9	£9.99
Oxfordshire (pb)	1-85937-430-1	£9.99	West Sussex	1-85937-148-5	£14.99
Peak District (pb)	1-85937-280-5	£9.99	West Yorkshire (pb)	1-85937-201-5	£9.99
Penzance	1-85937-069-1	£12.99	Weymouth (pb)	1-85937-209-0	£9.99
Peterborough (pb)	1-85937-219-8	£9.99	Wiltshire (pb)	1-85937-277-5	£9.99
Piers	1-85937-237-6	£17.99	Wiltshire Churches (pb)	1-85937-171-x	£9.99
Plymouth	1-85937-119-1	£12.99	Wiltshire Living Memories	1-85937-245-7	£14.99
Poole & Sandbanks (pb)	1-85937-251-1	£9.99	Winchester (pb)	1-85937-428-x	£9.99
Preston (pb)	1-85937-212-0	£9.99	Windmills & Watermills	1-85937-242-2	£17.99
Reading (pb)	1-85937-238-4	£9.99	Worcester (pb)	1-85937-165-5	£9.99
Romford (pb)	1-85937-319-4	£9.99	Worcestershire	1-85937-152-3	£14.99
Salisbury (pb)	1-85937-239-2	£9.99	York (pb)	1-85937-199-x	£9.99
Scarborough (pb)	1-85937-379-8	£9.99	Yorkshire (pb)	1-85937-186-8	£9.99
St Albans (pb)	1-85937-341-0	£9.99	Yorkshire Living Memories	1-85937-166-3	£14.99

See Frith books on the internet www.francisfrith.co.uk

FRITH PRODUCTS & SERVICES

Francis Frith would doubtless be pleased to know that the pioneering publishing venture he started in 1860 still continues today. A hundred and forty years later, The Francis Frith Collection continues in the same innovative tradition and is now one of the foremost publishers of vintage photographs in the world. Some of the current activities include:

Interior Decoration

Today Frith's photographs can be seen framed and as giant wall murals in thousands of pubs, restaurants, hotels, banks, retail stores and other public buildings throughout the country. In every case they enhance the unique local atmosphere of the places they depict and provide reminders of gentler days in an increasingly busy and frenetic world.

Product Promotions

Frith products are used by many major companies to promote the sales of their own products or to reinforce their own history and heritage. Frith promotions have been used by Hovis bread, Courage beers, Scots Porage Oats, Colman's mustard, Cadbury's foods, Mellow Birds coffee, Dunhill pipe tobacco, Guinness, and Bulmer's Cider.

Genealogy and Family History

As the interest in family history and roots grows world-wide, more and more people are turning to Frith's photographs of Great Britain for images of the towns, villages and streets where their ancestors lived; and, of course, photographs of the churches and chapels where their ancestors were christened, married and buried are an essential part of every genealogy tree and family album.

Frith Products

All Frith photographs are available Framed or just as Mounted Prints and Posters (size 23 x 16 inches). These may be ordered from the address below. From time to time other products - Address Books, Calendars, Table Mats, etc - are available.

The Internet

Already twenty thousand Frith photographs can be viewed and purchased on the internet through the Frith websites and a myriad of partner sites.

For more detailed information on Frith companies and products, look at these sites:

www.francisfrith.co.uk
www.francisfrith.com
(for North American visitors)

See the complete list of Frith Books at:

www.francisfrith.co.uk

This web site is regularly updated with the latest list of publications from the Frith Book Company. If you wish to buy books relating to another part of the country that your local bookshop does not stock, you may purchase on-line.

For further information, trade, or author enquiries please contact us at the address below:
The Francis Frith Collection, Frith's Barn, Teffont, Salisbury, Wiltshire, England SP3 5QP.
Tel: +44 (0)1722 716 376 Fax: +44 (0)1722 716 881 Email: sales@francisfrith.co.uk

See Frith books on the internet www.francisfrith.co.uk

TO RECEIVE YOUR FREE MOUNTED PRINT

Mounted Print
Overall size 14 x 11 inches

Cut out this Voucher and return it with your remittance for £1.95 to cover postage and handling, to UK addresses. For overseas addresses please include £4.00 post and handling. Choose any photograph included in this book. Your SEPIA print will be A4 in size, and mounted in a cream mount with burgundy rule line, overall size 14 x 11 inches.

Order additional Mounted Prints at HALF PRICE (only £7.49 each*)

If there are further pictures you would like to order, possibly as gifts for friends and family, purchase them at half price (no additional postage and handling required).

Have your Mounted Prints framed*

For an additional £14.95 per print you can have your chosen Mounted Print framed in an elegant polished wood and gilt moulding, overall size 16 x 13 inches (no additional postage and handling required).

---

* IMPORTANT!
These special prices are only available if ordered using the original voucher on this page (no copies permitted) and at the same time as your free Mounted Print, for delivery to the same address

---

Frith Collectors' Guild

From time to time we publish a magazine of news and stories about Frith photographs and further special offers of Frith products. If you would like 12 months FREE membership, please return this form.

Send completed forms to:
**The Francis Frith Collection,
Frith's Barn, Teffont, Salisbury,
Wiltshire SP3 5QP**

Voucher for FREE and Reduced Price Frith Prints

Picture no.	Page number	Qty	Mounted @ £7.49	Framed + £14.95	Total Cost
		1	**Free of charge***	£	£
			£7.49	£	£
			£7.49	£	£
			£7.49	£	£
			£7.49	£	£
			£7.49	£	£

Please allow 28 days for delivery   *** Post & handling**   **£3.50**

Book Title . . . .   **Total Order Cost**   **£**

Please do not photocopy this voucher. Only the original is valid, so please cut it out and return it to us.

I enclose a cheque / postal order for £ . . . .
made payable to 'The Francis Frith Collection'
OR please debit my Mastercard / Visa / Switch / Amex card
(credit cards please on all overseas orders)

Number . . . .

Issue No(Switch only) . . . . .Valid from (Amex/Switch) . . . .

Expires . . . .   Signature . . . .

Name Mr/Mrs/Ms . . . .

Address . . . .

. . . .

. . . . Postcode . . . .

Daytime Tel No . . . .

VALID TO 31/12/05

The Francis Frith Collectors' Guild

Please enrol me as a member for 12 months free of charge.

Name Mr/Mrs/Ms . . . .

Address . . . .

. . . .

. . . .

. . . . Postcode . . . .

Would you like to find out more about Francis Frith?

We have recently recruited some entertaining speakers who are happy to visit local groups, clubs and societies to give an illustrated talk documenting Frith's travels and photographs. If you are a member of such a group and are interested in hosting a presentation, we would love to hear from you.

Our speakers bring with them a small selection of our local town and county books, together with sample prints. They are happy to take orders. A small proportion of the order value is donated to the group who have hosted the presentation. The talks are therefore an excellent way of fundraising for small groups and societies.

Can you help us with information about any of the Frith photographs in this book?

We are gradually compiling an historical record for each of the photographs in the Frith archive. It is always fascinating to find out the names of the people shown in the pictures, as well as insights into the shops, buildings and other features depicted.

If you recognize anyone in the photographs in this book, or if you have information not already included in the author's caption, do let us know. We would love to hear from you, and will try to publish it in future books or articles.

Our production team

Frith books are produced by a small dedicated team at offices in the converted Grade II listed 18th-century barn at Teffont near Salisbury, illustrated above. Most have worked with the Frith Collection for many years. All have in common one quality: they have a passion for the Frith Collection. The team is constantly expanding, but currently includes:

Jason Buck, John Buck, Douglas Burns, Heather Crisp, Lucy Elcock, Isobel Hall, Rob Hames, Hazel Heaton, Peter Horne, James Kinnear, Tina Leary, Hannah Marsh, Eliza Sackett, Terence Sackett, Sandra Sanger, Lewis Taylor, Shelley Tolcher, Helen Vimpany, Clive Wathen and Jenny Wathen.